Living with Limpy

This is Frank Cachia's first book, another book about budgerigars followed shortly after.

Entitled "Living with a Budgerigar" it is all about Owning, Understanding and Interacting with a Budgerigar.

Living with Limpy

The true story of a relationship between a crippled owner and his crippled bird

Frank Cachia

Copyright © 2014 Frank Cachia

All rights are reserved. The material contained within this book is protected by copyright law, no part may be copied, reproduced, presented, stored, communicated or transmitted in any form by any means without prior written permission.

r90s@ozemail.com.au

A Catalogue-in-Publication is available from the National Library of Australia.

ISBN: 978-0-9941509-0-5

2nd Edition

Acknowledgement

Thanks to family and friends who encouraged and supported me while writing of this book

A special thanks to Dianne Mollison for her patience when it came to proof reading

The budgerigar, a loving creature, few ever regret owning one.

Frank Cachia

Prologue

When I was 10 years old my father bought me a pair of budgerigars. I named them Snowy, due to the white colour, and Sunny, due to the yellow colour. Many an hour was spent watching them as they hopped and briefly flew about in the rather large cage that dad constructed. They didn't stay around long, one day I forgot to close the door and in a flash without saying goodbye they flew away. I looked up and called out their names in between short crying bouts. They never came back. Well that friendship didn't last long. The day after, I went about playing with my train set. Within a week I forgot all about them.

Forty years later I found myself once again owning a budgerigar. I moved house, because I used to live practically next door to a hospital. Night and day all I heard was the slamming of car doors, the sounding of car horns, and ambulance sirens, and the occasional helicopter. There were always continuous background noises. My new house was in a quiet leafy no-through road. It was going from one extreme to another. Imagine hearing the sound of a plate shattering on a tiled floor from the next door neighbour's kitchen. Imagine waking up and, whilst rubbing one's eyes, you could hear the unmistakeable ticking sound of the kitchen clock. The deafening silence was unnerving.

At the beginning of 2000 I was visiting a friend when low and behold his son Nick, walked in with a budgie on his shoulder. What a lovely thing to see. Well that certainly brought back childhood memories. I turned my attention towards the son and talked about his birds. By the end of that visit I had arranged to buy one bird from him. The bird was to be delivered by the weekend.

I had no idea on how to train a bird but at the same time I didn't want to make him perform any tricks. What I wanted was to hear a bird's chirping to break up the silence, he could live his life, and I mine. What would be nice, what would be a bonus, was if he could eat from my hand and perhaps even sit on my shoulder?

When the bird was delivered I named him Bluey due to the fact that he was blue in colour. He lived in a cage in the kitchen. In time I opened the cage door and he spent time on the kitchen radio. Come night time and he flew back into his cage. As time passed and he got used to me, he briefly around breakfast time stayed on my finger or shoulder. Eventually while I had my breakfast, he did fly and ate some seeds off my hand. It was a treat for me to see him place one foot on the kitchen counter and another foot on my hand as he helped himself to the seeds. That was the only time we met during the day and this routine continued daily till one day just on four years later he passed away.

Six months passed before I bought another budgie this time from a pet store. Similar in colour as Bluey I named the new budgie Indi, short for Indian because of his colour scheme under his eyes. He reminded me of the American Indians, the way they wear war paint under their eyes in the old Hollywood movies. I was surprised to see Indi's behaviour was the same as Bluey, flying onto the kitchen radio, spending most of the time there and eating from my hands at the kitchen table. Regrettably he flatly refused to stay on my finger or shoulder.

The day my mum's funeral was taking place was also the day Indi passed away. It was the only time I wasn't paying much attention, I was running around dressing, waiting for my cousins to show up to take to the church and I left the toilet seat open. Indi flew in and drowned in the toilet bowl. I only had him for 6 months.

On the way to mum's funeral my cousin's stated that her son Tony was a budgerigar breeder didn't help, I just didn't want to know about budgies at all.

Chapter 1

An invitation to my cousin a month later, to see his budgies changed my outlook again. Standing in a garage with close to a hundred budgies in all their colourful noisy glory brought back a smile. I just went over to each cage whistling and talking to them. I just laughed observing their antics. Yep, there was no doubt about it, I wanted another budgie. Turning round I asked my cousin to sell me one. He said that he'll do so once some new ones are born. I agreed and went home shortly after.

One day, at the start of spring he rang me and said that he had a lovely blue budgie picked out and would call me at the appropriate time. More waiting, I mumbled to myself. Finally, the day came when I picked up the phone and heard him say that my budgie was now ready to be picked up and I should come over on the Thursday, Friday or the Saturday. I said that I would be there on Sunday. He disagreed and said that it had to be one of those three days because that would be the day when the window was open. I nominated Friday night. When I put the phone down I wondered what he is talking about, window, what window?

On 8th September 2006 I arrived at my cousin's place leaning to one side thanks to the heavy weight of the cage I was given when I picked up Bluey. Whoever built that cage wanted it to last forever. I'm sure it could survive a nuclear blast.

Upon entering the lounge room I saw my cousin holding a blue budgie and was gently scratching the area behind his head. I was surprised to see the bird passively letting such action take place. Relieved of the cage, I sat down next to him and asked Tony to explain what he was doing. He told me that budgies love to have the back of the head scratched. I understood and made a mental note to one day carry out such an act.

> Budgies in general do not like to be held. When the budgie is placed in one's hands he'll loudly screech. He fears that the enclosing hand is a predator's mouth. Another reason for screeching is because to the budgie, human skin feels quite alien.

It was then that I remembered the question I wanted to ask. "By the way Tony, on the phone you said something about a window. What are you talking about, window, what window?"

Tony turned and looking at me said "Irrespective whether a person wants a bird to train or simply as a house pet, the best time to get him is when the budgie has become independent from his parents but before he becomes completely independent from anyone and everyone. That period of time, that "open window" is a crucial three to five day period. Once that time frame is over he can still be trained but it gets slightly harder as the days go by. A breeder, a knowledgeable breeder, should keep an eye on the bird's behaviour and would know when the time is right for parental separation and owner introduction".

I wasn't going to argue with him. He was given a budgerigar as a birthday present on his twelfth birthday. He bought another budgie shortly after and once the hen dropped a couple of eggs Tony were so fascinated that he became a breeder. That was 35 years ago, so he certainly knew what he was talking about.

Tony slowly passed the budgie over. I gently took hold of him and under his direction, started to scratch the back of his head. There's no doubt about it he was enjoying the scratching sensation. "Well mate, it seems that we're going to get along just fine" I softly said. A few minutes later Tony commented about the cage weight as he brought it over and I put the budgie in it. The cage was placed in the back seat of the car and securely tied down. If any policeman saw me drive that night he would come to the conclusion that I was a careful driver accelerating and braking as gently as it was humanly possible. It was one very comfortable smooth ride that bird experienced.

The one advantage that the cage offered was that three sides of it were closed so it was easy to cover much of the front section with an old towel. The cage was placed on the kitchen table which was moved against the wall. A towel was placed further blocking the kitchen light and I moved into the study. Only the night light bathed the kitchen so I was quite sure that with hardly a sound in the house the bird would soon settle down and go to sleep.

Living with Limpy

The idea of sleeping in on Saturday was easily dismissed. I got out of bed and following the usual shower, shave and tooth brushing tip toed towards the kitchen saying "G'day" to my new mate. Halfway down the hall I came to a sudden stop. Just round the corner I could hear the bird merrily chirping. "I don't believe it" I muttered, "surely he couldn't have settled in already?" I walked into the kitchen and slowly so as not to startle him removed and folded the towel. I backed away and very briefly whistled. I smiled as I saw him up on a perch close to the cage door rather than at the back end of the cage. I prepared breakfast, switched on the radio and sat down to breakfast and, of course, just ready to watch him. During breakfast I placed seeds and water containers on the bottom of the cage whilst repeatedly whistling at him. I broadly smiled when he jumped down and helped himself to the water but was disappointed when he didn't touch any of the seeds.

During the morning as I went about doing some chores I kept peeking in but at no time were the seeds disturbed. "Something's wrong," I said, so I quickly reached for the phone and called Tony. As soon as I finished telling him why I rang he asked me what type of seeds I was offering. "I don't know the name; I just gave him the same seeds which I gave to Bluey and Indi." When he asked me where I got them from I replied "from the supermarket, where else" Tony laughed and said that I should go to a pet shop and buy canary plain seeds. I was quite surprised to hear him say that but he assured me to do just that. Once again I said "OK you're know best, see you later" and rushed back into the bedroom, changed clothes and drove down to the large 'Fish and Feathers' pet store just down the road from my place.

There was an instant response; within a moment of replacing the seeds he jumped onto my finger and than on the container. That surprised me. A second later he was head down and bum up rapidly feasting. Well that certainly told me what he likes. I threw away what was left of the supermarket seed and filling the empty container with the new seed.

Lunch was once again eaten while observing the bird. I was again surprised by his chirping. He hasn't even been here a day yet, and has already settled in, merrily chirping away. Yes, it is time to open the cage door and let him out. Seeing a bird in flight is a wonderous thing. I was never happy seeing a bird couped up in a cage, it's like placing him in a prison. I got up, closed the curtains and the kitchen window blind. I didn't want him to fly towards the window and then crash into it. As I got closer to him to open the cage door I suddenly noticed his left leg. I hadn't noticed that before, his toe arrangement was slightly deformed.

The most common arrangement of digits in birds are with three toes facing forward and one facing back. The budgie on the other hand has two toes facing forward and two facing back. His left leg has two toes facing forward, another facing back but the third digit is facing forward and is floppy as if it was connected only by the skin. When I slowly moved a finger towards the cage door he backed away and could then clearly see that the third digit wasn't moving with the rest, it was trailing behind. I was quite upset, wondering if he in pain, what should I do? I could ring up Tony but than again what could he do? Eventually I did ring him; he was surprised about it, because he had not noticed anything. "There's no much I can do" he said but did promise to pop over as soon as he had the time. Placing the phone back on the hook I walked back to the cage and spent time just observing the bird.

It was at this time that I realised I still hadn't named the budgie and decided I did not want to keep calling him 'bird'. His grip was unaffected he was quite able to grip the cage surrounds or any of the two perches with ease. What was noticeable when he walked along the water container was a slight limp on the left leg. Well there was the answer right in front of me; his limp identified him; Limpy. Yes, quite an appropriate name. And so from that moment onwards he was known as "Limpy".

Of course calling him by name didn't mean he would come over, in time he came over when he wanted to, not when I said so.

There are times when budgerigars balance on one leg when stretching and Limpy was no exception. When he did stretch he did it very cautiously. It is OK when he stretches his left leg because he's supporting himself on his good leg but at times he used to lose balance and fall over when he tried to hold himself up on the left leg.

Looking around once more, confirming that the curtains and kitchen blind were still closed, I turned around, faced the cage and said "OK Limpy, time to open up the cage door. You're more than welcomed to come out whenever you feel like it"

Living with Limpy

G'day, my name is Limpy – (Notice my defining feature!)

I opened the cage door and positioned myself out of his field of vision so as not to alarm him. Sitting down in the lounge room I picked up a book and once in a while looked up at the cage. I was very surprised because it didn't take long for him to act. Much to my surprise, I saw a head pop out; look both ways as if to cross the road and a moment later Limpy took flight heading straight onto a small radio placed on the kitchen window sill. A moment later he was walking along the top of the radio, pecking at the controls, inspecting every part of the surface and than started to chirp once again. In the next hour he flew around landing on top of the pantry, the top of the fridge, a small table against the wall, the kitchen counter and back to the radio.

Jumping down onto the window sill he came against the small section of window pane that wasn't covered by the blind. He chirped and tried to walk through but off course the glass held him back. Clearly one could see Limpy trying to move forward only to be stopped by the glass. A moment later he flew around landed back on the kitchen radio and stayed there.

All this time I was watching from the lounge room and decided to go to the kitchen, open the fridge, get a drink and walk back. I wanted to know how he would behave in my presence. Walking at a slower pace I entered the kitchen, approached and opened the fridge to retrieve a drink, all the time looking at Limpy. I started to laugh, doing my best to suppress it so as not to startle him. All that Limpy did was tilt his head from side to side while looking at me. He didn't move about, just kept at eye on me. He stood his ground on the radio without breaking eye contact - and most likely wondered who or what I was.

As the subdued sunlight started to diminish Limpy spend considerable time flying around the kitchen again landing on the same surfaces as before, finally ending back on the radio. He did fly back to the cage for some seeds and water and than back onto the radio. That surprised me, I wasn't expecting that. It's quite clear that he's comfortable being on the radio – even though he's already tripping over the various knobs and dials.

After I had finished my dinner I approached the wash basin to do the washing up. Limpy flew off landing on top of the pantry and stayed there. When I turned in that night he was still on top of the pantry.

Chapter 2

Guess what, he was still there when I showed up again the following morning. His eyes never left me, he followed my every step. When I went to replenish his water I absentmindedly left the container out on the small table. Limpy flew down helped himself to a drink and once again flew back up to the pantry. I switched on the radio and decided to walk away and moved into the lounge room. Hardly had I sat down when Limpy flew down landing on the radio and within a minute started to chirp along with the music. As soon as I approached the radio he took flight landing back on top of the pantry.

I wondered, talking out loud. "He flew down for the water, what about some seeds" I picked some and showed him a handful of seeds. He was obviously very interested by the amount of head tilting. It didn't take long before he flew down onto my hand helped himself to the seeds, than completely surprised me by casually walking onto my shoulder and started to groom himself. This wasn't supposed to happen this way and so soon I thought. Bluey and Indi never did this. Turning my head to look at him he briefly stopped grooming, looked at me and a moment later started his grooming again. I was afraid to move, I didn't want to disturb him. I slowly walked to the lounge room, sat down and picked up the book from where I had left off, and started to read.

How could I read, how could I concentrate, here I sat with a bird on my shoulder that had been with me for just over a day, busily grooming himself. I tried and succeeded in relaxing ever so slowly moving my back against the back of the settee. I managed to read a paragraph and slowly turn over the page, while the budgerigar was busily turning himself inside out bending into impossible angles as he cleaned himself. I couldn't help it; I started to laugh, especially when I saw him rapidly move his head back against the tail bone.

Living with Limpy

> Budgerigars possess an oil gland at the base of their tail. Throwing their heads back they rub their beak on this, collect some oil and use this over their feathers for waterproofing, cleaning and of course to smooth down the feathers.

It was really fascinating watching his comical antics. But it wasn't, when at one stage he moved and sent his tail straight into my ear lobe. I had an overwhelming desire to chase it with my finger but I managed to resist.

When he had finished he took off returning to the radio. I stood up, picked up his seed container threw out all the seeds and replenished it. Instead of placing the container back in the cage I placed it next to the water container on the small table. Going to the garage, I picked up a cardboard box lid placed it on the small table, and placed both containers there.

After lunch I raised the kitchen window blind up by a few inches letting more light in to the room. That movement startled Limpy. When a bird is startled he always fly to a higher plain to get out of danger. This is normal bird behaviour. Not Limpy, he flew onto my shoulder, ran and hid behind my neck. He was afraid; he actually positioned me between the moving blind and himself. I was lost for words. This bird was surprising me with every movement; this wasn't supposed to happen, his actions weren't text book behaviour.

After a few minutes on my shoulder I slowly moved my finger towards Limpy hoping he would jump onto my finger. He didn't, and instantly took off landing back on the radio. I repeated the same whistle I had when I replaced his food and water containers. I moved about the kitchen and every few seconds whistled the same short tune. After a few times I stopped moving about, leaned down supporting myself against the kitchen counter and again started to whistle. This went on till my lips were dry. I stopped for a drink and than moved the glass slowly towards Limpy. Imagine the joy when he reached over and took a sip of water from my glass. I loved it, this was great. I decided to once again try to see if he would get on my finger.

I slowly approached him again extending a finger hoping once again that he'd jump on it. Alas, he again took off circling around the kitchen landing on the kitchen counter. Well, I wouldn't exactly call it a good landing. As a matter of fact I would go so far as to say that it was the worst landing so far. Limpy had mastered the art of flying. Although sometimes one can see a slight doubt, once his legs spring up, the take off has been text book perfect, however his landings at times do leave a lot to be desired and this was no exception. Limpy

Living with Limpy

Slowly, very slowly move a finger towards him. Never make any sudden moves. Once a bird gains the owner's trust place the finger very close to his chest and he will climb onto the finger. It does take time and requires patience. Note: Just as the bird climbs onto a finger there's also the desire to fly away.

Hint: Move the finger close enough to touch a mirror. This will cause the bird to start looking at his 'new mate' and will be so absorbed that he'll forget he's on a human finger. Without realising it he'll accept and will be comfortable being on this new 'perch'.

---

came in with his undercarriage stretched out ready for a perfect two point landing but the smooth bench top surface was slippery, resulting in Limpy skidding sideways and sliding past me crashing into the toaster.

There's no doubt in my mind that he was not amused because a moment later quite a few irritating chirps could loudly be heard. Doing my utmost to control my side splitting laughter I lent a hand or should say provide a finger for him to right himself up. And it was at that exact moment that Limpy climbed onto my finger. Again he surprised me because this wasn't the way it is supposed to happen. I managed to slow down my laughter and marvelled at this bird. A moment later as I straightened up I moved my finger forward and once again he jumped onto the radio.

Supervising all kitchen activities from atop the radio

Not letting the moment pass I presented my finger moving it very close to his chest and he jumped on. I was so elation. I moved my other hand once again presenting a finger and he climbed onto it. I started to move alternative fingers each time he climbed onto it. This action looked very similar to Limpy climbing a ladder. While I was doing these manoeuvres I also slowly turned a full circle seeing whether that would in any way distract him. It didn't, so I slowly walked into the dining room followed by the lounge room and sat down in front of the TV.

Feeling confident, I slowly moved my right arm with Limpy still on the straightened out finger towards my left shoulder but stopping way before the finger touched it. While moving the arm back and forth I replayed the same whistle as before. All this time Limpy was just standing there looking at me. I wished I knew what he was thinking; most likely wondering what is the matter with me. As my arm started to tire, I moved it closer to the shoulder until it got close enough for him to jump onto my shoulder. You should have seen the smile on my face. I turned to look at him just in time to once again see him groom himself.

When a budgerigar is sitting on a person's shoulder and starts to groom himself that clearly shows he trusts the person.

I decided to let him be. I just slowly crossed my legs, leant back, made a note of the time and switched on the TV. Twenty minutes were to pass before Limpy took off, once again flying towards the kitchen and the radio. Shortly after, he flew over to the edge of the counter, looked around as if he was inspecting the area and feeling safe flew down to the cardboard lip, and hopped down to the water and food containers.

As the day progressed Limpy spent time on the radio, flying onto the top of the pantry and onto the fridge. Chirping was often heard. As the day came to a close I switched on the kitchen light and also lowered the blind. I didn't lower it all the way because it would have been in his way while he was on the radio. Presenting him with a finger he once again jumped on it. "Time for you to turn in for the night mate", I gently whispered. "Where do you want to sleep tonight, the top of the pantry or back in the cage?" Well I couldn't reach the pantry top so I took him to the cage. Limpy dutifully landed on the cage entrance, I turned around and he flew back on my shoulder. I just broke up laughing, what do I do? A few minutes later he took off and went back to the radio. "OK," I said to him, "stay there". What else could I say?

Living with Limpy

Finishing from the kitchen I switched the light off and went back to watch TV. As I sat there, I decided to show Limpy the rest of the house. I would be much happier if he found another room to sleep in. He couldn't sleep in the kitchen, for as soon as I walked in for whatever reason, he would wake up. I didn't particularly want to disturb his sleep.

I was quite surprised when I walked into the kitchen the following morning to once again see Limpy on the kitchen radio. My first question was – did he stay there or did he retire back into the cage. A quick inspection showed that there were no droppings inside the cage but a few on the paper next to the radio.

I once again approached him while whistling the same tune. Presenting my finger I was surprised to see how easily he jumped on to it. As a matter of fact I would say that he flew on to it. I said the usual "G'day" and after switching on the kettle, turned around to retrieve sliced bread plus milk and butter. Limpy walked up my arm, watching my every move as I replenished his feed and water. He then moved further up all the way to my shoulder and with intense curiosity watched me prepare coffee and some toast.

It was quite a novelty moving about the kitchen and having Limpy on my shoulder. As usual I switched on the radio and enjoyed breakfast while listening to the Neil Mitchell talk back radio programme.

Hardly had I sat down at the table when all of a sudden, I saw a blur of blue and Limpy running down my shoulder, hopping onto the table and approaching the plate. Right there in front of my eyes he took a tiny nibble of the vegemite toast. I just looked at him; I didn't know budgies liked vegemite. He turned around and walked away then spun right round again and went back for another nibble. I just looked at him with a bemused smile. It was unmistakeable, here's a budgerigar sampling a new food, clearly seeing his tongue move about while once again taking another tiny nibble. I looked around, where's my camera? Why isn't there anyone around seeing what I'm seeing so as to have a witness? A moment later the tiny nibble changed to "this is yummy" and he just went ahead and helped himself. I didn't know whether it was good for him, I didn't know whether his metabolism could handle such an item. As a precaution I pulled the toast away. There's no doubt in my mind, Limpy didn't like this action because he let out one single ear piercing shrill. As soon as I started to lower the toast down to the table again, he approached it and once he was within reach started to pick on it again.

Hardly had I stopped shaking my head, when he stopped, jumped back onto my hand and casually, as if he had all the time in the world, walked back to my shoulder.

I turned to face him to ask "finished? When all of a sudden I completely loss control and broke up laughing. Limpy just stared at me possibly wondering what the matter was with me, but again as soon as I looked back at him I just continued laughing my head off. Off course he couldn't see it; Limpy's beak tip had a minute smear of vegemite. It looked like he was wearing a gentleman's pencil thin moustache. How could I possible keep a straight face?

By the time I wiped my eyes and calmed down both the coffee and toast were cold. The table once cleared, Limpy was back on the radio. I started to laugh again, watching him clean his beak against his chest feathers and then cleaning up his feathers. Is this bird using this technique to briefly save some vegemite to 'have it later' or is it a case of getting him to wear a bib?

When one observes a bird just finish eating or drinking their next move is always the cleaning of their beaks. Wild birds would usually use any item such as the top of a wooden fence or a tree branch and then move their beaks in a zigzag formation each time caressing their beaks against the item at hand thus removing any tiny pieces of food from their beaks. This action is usually shown by their elders thus the young ones learn through copying them.

Limpy is a bird, that either was never shown, or never bothered to imitate the elders. Later that morning I observed him eating some seeds, and when he finished eating didn't bother to clean his beak at all. He indifferently walked to the water container with a couple of seed husks still stuck to his beak. He made no attempt whatsoever to dislodge them. When it came to having a drink, the only thing he didn't do was blow bubbles. He nearly dunked his whole head in the water. Although he drank as normally as possible, he actually shook off any water droplets whilst still having his beak in the water. I've never seen a bird behave in such a manner, sloppy, very sloppy. Limpy didn't believe in any table manners, a complete slob.

He flew around but apart from a dash to the top of the cage he stayed in the kitchen. Come lunch time and fruit was the order of the day. As I was cutting an apple on the kitchen counter Limpy flew down and hurriedly approached the cut slices. Great I thought, he love fruit. It didn't last; he moved about the slices and promptly walked to the knife. As soon as he saw his reflections he started to chirp. I left him, placed a slice of bread in the toaster, then spread vegemite and instantly Limpy made a beeline for it. No goodbye to his mate in the reflection, he had just one thing in mind – food. I had the strangest feeling that as long as I offer him vegemite, I'm his best mate. As soon as I removed it he once again let out one single ear piercing shrill.

G'day mate

I don't know whether I should be happy that I now knew what a single shrill stands for, or whether to rejoice that I have found a way to get him to follow me. I went to the garage and came back with an old shaving mirror and set it up on top of the refrigerator.

Getting Limpy to once again get on my finger I approached the mirror. As soon as he saw his own reflection he walked toward it and started to chirp. His chirping sometimes loud sometimes soft was unending. I don't know what he was saying but he certainly made sure that his new friend heard him. I enjoyed a light lunch observing Limpy's actions at the mirror. This is better than watching TV, no commercials.

In the afternoon I again had Limpy on my finger and took him around, showing him all the rooms in the house. I was hoping upon hope that he would select a room where I wouldn't be able to disturb him. He stayed on my finger in both the study and computer games room. A walk down the corridor to the laundry and visitor's toilet didn't produce any positive results either. Thankfully the same went for the dinning and lounge rooms. I took him to the visitor's bathroom hoping upon hope that with the large mirror above the wash basin he would fly over to it. Alas, same result. Bloody hell how fussy is this bird? All that was left was my bedroom and the on-suite. Sure enough he showed no interest in the bedroom but as soon as we approached the on-suite he took off heading straight for the towel rack. Well that's great but I didn't know whether I should be happy or not. This meant that taking a shower before turning in, means that he'll be waking up again. I didn't know whether to be happy or not. On one hand Limpy has selected a room to make his own; however on the other hand this meant that I would have to use the visitor's bathroom for my nightly shower. When or if I wake up in the middle of the night I would have to walk to the other side of the house to the visitor's toilet so as not to disturb him.

Well, I certainly got the short end of the stick.

Limpy made himself at home in the bathroom, on the few times I went to see what he was up to I saw him flying to the top of the shower frame or the old "Realistic" radio placed on the bathroom window sill or onto the mirror frame saying 'G'day' to and making a new friend in that mirror.

Later that day I saw him fly into the bedroom and back to the bathroom. Around dusk I went to him and presenting a finger to get on to, took him to the kitchen where he flew over to the food and water containers. Once he finished I took him back to the bathroom where he instantly flew from me, once again landing on the towel rack. As the room got darker the chirping slowed down.

Living with Limpy

A radio loving budgie – I moved the toothbrush out of his reach because he wouldn't leave it alone.

Chapter 3

Being woken up by an alarm clock is one thing; being woken up by the sounds of a budgerigar chirping is another? This was the case one morning. I slowly turned over looking up at the ceiling enjoying such a sweet melody. The chirping just went on and on. I slowly sat up in bed afraid that any movement would cause him to stop. Slowly practically holding my breath in fear of making any noise I leaned forward and saw Limpy on the towel rack merrily chirping away. When I stood up and walked into the bathroom he stopped. He held his ground, didn't move from the towel rack but didn't take his eyes off me either. By the position of his droppings on an old towel placed on the floor, it was quite evident that he slept there all night. That towel came in handy because when I opened the shower door, water drips on the floor. Now it was doing double duty. He only moved flying to the bathroom radio, only when I pulled the towel to dry myself. Shaving and teeth brushing was carried out under his watchful eyes.

After I dressed I approached him and he eagerly jumped on my finger. As I approached the kitchen he took off landing back on the kitchen radio. This bird had a thing for radios. As the kettle was pressed into service I changed his feed and replaced the water. Once again he surprised me by flying onto my hand, and approaching the container had his fill of fresh aerated water. As soon as I placed the containers back in place he flew over, with water droplets still dripping from his beak, to the food container.

Breakfast was a copy of the previous day. As soon as Limpy spotted the toasted vegemite sliced bread he made a beeline for it. The toast was half way between the plate and my mouth. I had just enough time to hear a wing flap before a blurred bird flew by past the left side of my head and landed on my hand, and proceeded to feast on it. As I have already stated, absolutely no table manners whatsoever.

After breakfast Limpy spend time not only flying around the kitchen but also flying to the dining and the lounge room. This was definitely a case of spreading his wings. He was now beginning to explore his surroundings. By now having accepted the invisible barrier preventing him from flying further out from the window sill radio the kitchen blinds were fully opened. Meanwhile the cage was still there, empty; Limpy hadn't been in it once as far as I was aware. What an absolute joyous sight it was to see Limpy land on the radio and than take off at counter height level, wings flapping each stroke swinging a full arch. A few seconds later he climbed gaining height and landed on the lounge room curtain rod. A moment later he turned around and with a screech dove off the rod, and with a momentary glide, flapped his way back to the radio.

Clearly he's enjoying flying about.

Watching TV programmes are annoying when the ads come on; watching the same programme with a budgie flashing past was quite distracting. I didn't know whether to watch the TV or watch his fly-bys.

Whistling continued especially when I was very close to Limpy. Quite often I would present my finger and whistle. Limpy caught on and by early afternoon he would jump onto my extended finger. I than started to move my finger towards my shoulder and it didn't take long before Limpy jumped onto my shoulder. It was rather novel walking about the house with a bird on my left shoulder. I should have worn a patch over one eye and called myself a pirate. I had to laugh. I noticed that as long as I was walking Limpy was quite happy to be carried around, however once I stopped moving, he would simply take off. Clearly he was not patient.

It was then that I decided to walk around showing Limpy the flight path to take from the kitchen to the bathroom. If I was being spied upon, the person would have wondered why I was walking from the kitchen through the dining, lounge, cross the hallway to the bedroom and than the bathroom to then turn around and retrace my steps. I did this, walking back and forth quite a few times. In all this time Limpy stayed on my shoulder, looking and a chirp or two sounded like an acknowledgement. Whether he got fed up with the tour, or finally seeing his image in the bathroom mirror, I'll never know, but finally he took off, landing on the mirror's frame and started to have a chat to his mate in the mirror.

Living with Limpy

This is my bathroom mate – he's very argumentative

Tony rang asking me how the bird was settling in. I told him of what had been going on. He than informed me that he'd be able to pop over the following night.

Sitting in the lounge room I could hear Limpy chirping in the bathroom. Later on Limpy flew out from the bathroom flying through the bedroom and as soon as he saw me sitting down in the lounge room, landed on my shoulder. Hardly had I had time to turn around and "say g'day", and he once again took off through the dining room landing back on the kitchen radio. A moment later he flew to the edge of the kitchen counter looked around, made sure the coast was clear and then flew down to the cardboard lid where his food and water containers where. The tapping of his beak against the bowl surface told me that he was helping himself to a feed. As soon as he finished he stepped over to the water container. He once again flew onto the lip of the cardboard lid looked around and flew over onto my shoulder. Again I hardly had time to say g'day when he once again took off heading towards the bedroom and than the bathroom. Well that was certainly an exercise in flying; and I was the temporary stop over.

Where's Limpy? I suddenly realised that he hadn't been seen flying about or heard any chirping and it caused me to pause the DVD. As I stood up to go and look for him, I realised that the house was getting dark. I switched on the kitchen light and went looking for him. I wish I had had the camera with me; there was Limpy on the bathroom towel rack. As I got closer it was quite clear that he was about to close his eyes. "OK mate" I whispered, I'll let you go to sleep.

I returned back to check on him a few moments later. Yep, he was asleep. I returned back to the lounge and as I pressed play on the DVD, lowered the volume. Not wishing to disturb him when I turned in I tip toed into the bedroom, undressed in the dark and gently slid down under the covers. Again so as not to disturb him when I woke up in the middle of the night to go to the toilet, I tip toed out of the still darkened room and headed to the visitor's toilet on the other side of the house.

I woke up to the sound of chirping emanating from the bathroom. This is the second day that Limpy had slept in the bathroom. I got up and walked into the bathroom. Limpy was on the window sill radio, facing the frosted window, merrily chirping away to his heart's content. He stopped when he saw me, turned around and just sat there observing me. He hardly moved throughout my shower, shaving and tooth brushing.

When I finished from the bathroom I extended out my finger, he jumped on and moved him over onto my shoulder. Anyone observing this act would come to the conclusion that we have been doing this for quite some time. In actual fact it was the first time that this had happened without any hesitation from him. Back in the bedroom Limpy stayed on my shoulder observing me as I went about putting on my clothes.

Hardly had I arrived in the kitchen when he took off aiming straight at the kitchen radio. Once again I replaced his seed container. He watched me like a hawk; as soon as I replenished his water and presented it to him he flew onto my hand and helped himself to a drink. Well he's no dummy, aerated water tastes much better.

I decided not to have any toasted vegemite; instead I just buttered a couple of slices of bread and placed some sliced cheese over them. Limpy wasn't the slightest interested, that is, until I caught him helping himself to the tub of margarine. I didn't believe this. Here was a budgie balancing on the edge of a tub helping himself to the margarine. No, no, this is no good. I have never heard of a budgie eating margarine. This could be problematic, for all I knew his stomach might not be able to process it. I decided to put a stop to it. Reaching over and picking up the lid I proceeded to cover the tub. One single solitary loud shrill shattered the air, Limpy made it quite clear that my action was not acceptable. A moment later he started to flap his wings and screech. Still this must stop and with Limpy still trying to hold back my hand I covered the tub. Limpy registered his disapproval by loudly chirping, taking to the air, flying onto the kitchen radio, then off towards the bathroom.

Yummy – breakfast of champions

I had to laugh, how does one explain what has just happened? Tony was popping over that night, would I tell him that Limpy wants margarine or that he loudly objected to being stopped from having any. I walked over to the bathroom and Limpy was silently sitting on the radio looking at the frosted window. He didn't turn to face me. I didn't believe this. I had a budgie that had just thrown a tantrum and was giving me the silent treatment. What could I do other than laugh!

As the day progressed Limpy flew out of the bathroom, briefly landed on my shoulder then onto the kitchen, ate, drank, flew over once again onto my shoulder before returning back to the bathroom. In all this time did not bothered about the cage. I don't think he even looked at it let alone went or even slept inside it.

At dusk Tony rang informing me that take away fish and chips was on the menu that night. Shortly after, the sounds of a car door being slammed shut announced his arrival. Sitting down at the kitchen he proceeded to have his meal.

Out of the blue Limpy flew over landing next to the food. What was it with this bird; he was able to smell food from three rooms away? Tony looked at me saying that he was about to ask me about the bird and here he was moving about the French fries feeling his way around to the coolest ones. As soon as he found one he started to gently peck at it. We looked at each other in amazement. Is this a normal thing with budgies I asked? Do they like French fries? Tony shrugged his shoulder telling me with a puzzled look on his face that he has never seen this happen in all the years he has been breeding budgies. Once again we looked at Limpy casually walking about pecking at the fries. Even when Tony reached out for some of them Limpy didn't budge, he kept on moving about at his own pace. We just broke up laughing, how does one explain such animal behaviour?

When Limpy had his fill, he took off flying to his water bowl, drank and again with droplets dripping from his beak, flew away heading back to the bathroom. Lost for words we just shook our heads in utter disbelief. We discussed Limpy's behaviour, how easily he had settled down and due to his limp when he walked, his most appropriate name.

Tony led the way to the bathroom wanting to handle Limpy so he could examine his leg. It was quite clear to Limpy that having two towering human adults in his domain were not welcome. He loudly screeched as he reached for the highest point in the room. With the aid of a small towel Tony managed to capture Limpy and proceeded with an examination. We returned back to the kitchen with the last few rays of sunshine offering better lighting. Tony wasn't sure how the leg came to be as it was other than Limpy damaging it in infancy or just after he came to me. He said that as far as he knew when he had placed the leg tag, both feet looked normal. As there was nothing that could be done and clearly apart from his limp Limpy was behaving normally, we accepted what had happened.

I laughed asking Tony if it's normal for a budgie that loved vegemite and French fries? He just shook his head. A moment later Tony slowly opened his hand and we both watched Limpy fluff up and than take off.

When he flew off we expected Limpy to fly back to the bathroom, instead much to my surprise and Tony's bemused look, Limpy flew around, landing on my shoulder and ran around hiding behind my neck. Well this was the second time he had done this. You recall he ran and hid behind my neck when he positioned me between the moving kitchen blind and himself. He was scared then too. Now having 'escaped' from the stranger's clutching hand he flew over hiding behind my neck. He was safe there, since he couldn't see Tony, than to his logic Tony can't see him.

This was a learning curve and we did our best not to crack up laughing. Tony, while looking at my neck, assured me that there was nothing that could be done to remedy his leg. Whilst I was agreeing with him I could feel Limpy's nails digging into the skin at the back of my neck. A second later I saw Tony look towards the side of my neck and at the same time I could feel Limpy move. I just broke up laughing. Limpy was moving around to my right side approaching the shoulder looking to see if the big bad person was still there. As soon as Tony saw him peaking around my neck he started laughing. There's not much else one can do in this type of situation. Once Limpy saw him he again returned to the relative safety of my neck.

If you think I was lost for words you should have seen Tony. His facial expressions said it all. He said that in his 30 years of breeding budgies he had never heard of a budgie eating vegemite let alone one that hid. He said that budgies would usually just fly away. "Well he is certainly bonding with you, Frank"

In the following few days Limpy settled down into a routine of sharing my breakfast, spending time on the bathroom and kitchen radio, flying from the kitchen through the

> Birds will at time shake their bodies and feathers. This action helps them to capture air placing it between their body and feathers to either warm up or even cool down. They also do so after being held because they want to have their feathers re-aligned. It's like re-arranging ones clothes.

dining and lounge room to the bathroom via the bedroom and return, either coming and spending time on my shoulder or just flying over to make sure I was there, and then returning to the bathroom.

Limpy never bothered entering the cage. By the end of the week the cage was moved to the garage and placed in storage.

Chapter 4

My brother was born in a tent. There, I said it. He had too, tents do not have doors and I have never seen Les close a door behind him. Here we were in the kitchen looking at a budgie on the kitchen radio, and when Les directly entered the garage from the house, he left it wide open. It was infuriating. Returned holding a borrowed tool, and thanked me, then left the door wide open. Even before I had Limpy, everytime he came over and went into the garage no amount of bellowing "close the bloody door," made a difference. How both Bluey and Indi never flew off is a mystery?

All I do was either roll my eyes back, or simply just shake my head.

Limpy, whose behaviour even in such a short time clearly showed that he was vastly different the previous two birds had absolutely showed no interest in flying through? Mind you, with plenty of opportunity to indulge his love of vegemite, why leave? As they say – "If you're on a good thing stick to it".

So far I had left Limpy alone for only a brief period of time. I went out to do some shopping making sure that the house was 'safe'. This meant that all toilet seats were in the closed position, no windows or outside doors left open and any rooms that I did not want him in to have the door closed. Unfortunately the few days holiday was over and it was time to return back to work.

When it was time to depart I went around the house a number of times making sure that everything was in place and in 'budgie safe mode.' Just before I exited into the garage I switched on the radio.

Never had I spent a day looking at the clock, I just wanted to go home and see him again. I just wanted to make sure he was OK. This action surprised me because I hadn't acted in this way with either Bluey or Indi. Clearly there was no doubt that I had bonded more with Limpy than the other two. I

Living with Limpy

The Budgerigar is a social bird. He is by nature a gregarious creature and is often seen flying with others in either small or large flocks. Even in a pet store or in a house he's seen with others. However if he's by himself he does become and feel the loneliness. Since Limpy was for most part of the day going to be by himself I switched on the kitchen radio to keep him company.

gulped down my lunch as if to hurry up time. As soon as the time was right, I clocked off and practically ran to my car.

As soon as I walked into the house I whistled and started looking around. I didn't have to worry; Limpy was once again on the kitchen radio. I walked up to him, presented my finger and he hopped on. After repeating the same whistle a couple of times I placed him on my shoulder and walked into the bedroom. I was pleasantly surprised to see Limpy move about on me as I took off the clothes. Entering the bathroom he flew off onto the bathroom radio and stayed there as I showered. As soon as I walked out he flew back onto my shoulder and again, as I dressed, Limpy moved about on me. He stayed on the shoulder as I walked back into the kitchen. Inspecting his feed container showed empty seeds shells. Well I knew that he had eaten but how much?

Apart from food and water there's another item that some owners offer the budgie - Shell grit. The use of placing another container filled with shell grit is something that raises different opinions. As a matter of fact it does more than that. This is a rather argumentative issue among owners, breeders and veterinary staff. What is shell grit? More importantly why offer it?

Shell grit is grit from shells. It is also used as a source of calcium for birds. Why offer it?

In my case I did place a container of grit but seeing that Limpy didn't touch it, it was eventually removed months later.

The one thing that was consistent was whistling. As time passed Limpy recognised and associated with it. Every time I arrived back home from work I used to whistle the same tune as I approached him. I would quite often see him either on the kitchen or bathroom radio. All I did was approach him, present my finger and he would hop on it as soon as I whistled. That short tune was the first means of communicating. Whenever he stayed out 'late' and due to the lack of daylight was unable to fly back to the bathroom I

Budgies, when they are about to eat literally push seeds aside and pick up the seeds from the bottom of the pile. I decided to replace the feed container to a much flatter plastic dish. I placed the daily measured amount in the dish and then gently shook the dish so that all the seeds lie next to each other. This way no matter how much he pushed seeds around none were being flicked out which reduces any mess, but more importantly, I could clearly see how much he was eating. When at home I can hear the tap tapping sound made by the beak and so know that he's eating.

While I'm on the subject of eating and drinking one must keep in mind that water and feed should be replaced daily.

When looking at the seed dish some people actually make the mistake of saying that there's plenty of feed still present. This, most often, isn't the case. When the budgie splits the seed and eats it he'll leave the husk behind. The husk is the outer shell or coating of a seed. This of course is the remains of a seed and should be disposed off. It is far too big a task to separate the unopened seeds from those already eaten so simply empty the dish and replenish it with fresh seeds. I use a measuring cup and the amount of seeds thrown out is negligible. Dump the remains either in the rubbish bin or throw it in the back yard and you'll soon have wild birds helping themselves to a free meal.

Replacing the water is quite easy; however clean the container every few days. Run your finger around the bowl. If you feel a slippery surface that means that the bowl has a layer or a coating of 'slime' and should be removed. Still water does leave a 'ring' around the surface. That slime eventually will have algae. Clean it by rubbing it off with a finger; do not use any soap or chemicals. A simple wetting of paper towel after running it along the surface with a finger would suffice. You'll know it is clean because the surface isn't slippery anymore.

---

wouldn't even bother to present my finger for him to hop on to. All I did was to walk close to wherever he was standing and whistle, he would fly onto my shoulder and would continue on. Once I had arrived in the bathroom he would fly down to the towel rack and settle down on the towel.

Having the run of the house Limpy did explore opened rooms. However, within a short period he stopped visiting the visitor's bathroom and laundry. The only time he entered the study was when perched on my shoulder. I would sit in front of the computer and he would fly down onto the keyboard. He would explore and inspect whatever was on the desk. Nothing was ever left untouched, he had to investigate everything. Once satisfied he would take off and fly back to the kitchen.

A worker, any worker always looks forward towards the weekend; days off work can be spent doing other more enjoyable tasks. I was no exception; however all I wanted to do was to spend the day with Limpy. I found out that spending the time with him was quite informative, educational, very interesting and comical. By now his landings had immensely improved but there were still times that these landings deserved filming. The lounge room coffee table has a glass top. I was sitting down on the sofa with some photographs laid out on this table. Limpy's curiosity meant that he wanted to know what I was doing. Landing on my shoulder was by now a daily occurrence. This instance he decided to land on the table and walk among the photographs. Well his landing was satisfactory but with no traction whatsoever he skidded across and fell off the edge. What hope had I, to keep a straight face? As he madly chirped whilst gaining height, I started a hearty

---

A budgie eats by using the beak to split the seed, than swallows it whole, leaving the outer covering, the husk behind. That's all very well but the seed is swallowed whole, there's no chewing at all, there's no breaking down the seed. Shell grit helps in the digestion. Some seeds take a longer time to digest thus the continuous clashing of the grit against the seed will help the body absorb the nutrition.

The grit stays in the stomach for months on end. Eventually as it wears down it will harmlessly pass through the system. Once that happens the bird will ingest a couple of grit and start again.

Other animals use the same principal. One that comes to mind is the alligator. This creature will eat large pieces of meat. After the kill food is stuffed under a ledge to soften it. You see the alligator has a problem - he's unable to chew his food, he just swallows it whole. To help his stomach acids dissolve the food he picks up and swallow a couple of river rocks. These rocks sit in the stomach and with his body movement over time will help crush the food. Eventually he will pass out a rock or two. He might have the rocks for years before picking up more.

If you decide to supply your bird with grit, place it in another container. Do not mix it with his food. The bird chooses how much he wants and when he wants it. If he doesn't want any he doesn't take any. Some owners will not supply grit to their birds and some do, both for their own reasons. So decide for yourself.

laugh. Limpy landed on my shoulder and once again rushed over hiding behind my back.

Apart from me Limpy had only met Tony and because he had been caught and handled by him, Limpy's response was wary towards others. The next persons that Limpy met were my brother and nephew Adrian. Both presented a finger hoping that he would jump on, but only with Adrian. Both my brother Les and Tony and I are the same height but at the time Adrian was a good deal shorter. To Limpy, Adrian still towers over him yet seeing him from shoulder height he can see that Adrian is shorter. Is it possible that a bird would actually choose a person solely based on height? Well, for whatever reason Limpy hopped on Adrian's finger than walked up his arm onto his shoulder. Adrian was, of course happy about it. This was quite an unexpected event.

More friends met Limpy but much to their disappointment Limpy flatly refused to oblige their request and just stayed on my shoulder.

My cousin Mary Anne was one of the first to say g'day to Limpy. She was happy to see him approach her, walking along the couch back rest but much to her disappointment he kept her at arm's length.

Another visitor – no, I'm not going to jump on your finger or shoulder lady.

It was becoming quite clear that Limpy had bonded very strongly with me. Most of the time, as soon as he had a bite to eat or drink he would fly over onto my shoulder and carry out his preening. Watching his antics around the house or in front of a mirror were enjoyable and funny, but seeing him spend considerable time on my shoulder was even better, he was my little mate.

The only thing that I wasn't exactly happy with was Limpy's choice of food. His love of vegemite expanded to eating margarine either from my toast or directly from the tub. This soon extended to French Fries, mushroom soup, Chinese takeaway and even a forgotten cold cup of coffee. As soon as these items had started to cool off he helped himself. It was both amusing and disturbing to see him walk on the plate's edge feeling out any morsel that had cooled off. I knew that these items should not be on a bird's diet, so I restricted his movements by blocking his progress, but all I received was an objectionable shrill, loud enough to be heard from across the road. Limpy simply loved 'junk' food and avoided anything that was good for him, just like a teenager!

Tony suggested that I should offer Limpy some millet, a grain very much loved by small birds. When I got my hands on some, Limpy just wasn't interested. Fruit and vegetables were next on the menu but still I was out of luck. Whatever I presented Limpy stubbornly refused everything. Of course if I opened a jar of vegemite or a tub of margarine and left it on the kitchen counter, Limpy would just about bowl me over to get to it.

Searching around the World Wide Web for help I came across a budgie group, a group of like minded people who own budgerigars as pets or as breeders. http://pets.groups.yahoo.com/group/budgie-place/?yguid=1557628

I immediately joined. Over time many an email was exchanged passing on information about our feathered friends.

I implemented their food introduction suggestions but Limpy simply continued on having his way. Whoever said that a donkey was stubborn had never met Limpy.

About 3 months after Limpy entered my life, a mate suggested I should get another bird. When I asked him why, he replied that Limpy might be lonely and could do with a companion. I laughed replying that Limpy has a companion: me. From his point of view he hadn't asked for a companion because he already had one.

There's no problem whatsoever introducing another bird into the household, either for a breeding programme or just as another companion for either yourself or the first bird. However you must keep in mind that in introducing a third party other than for breeding purposes, the following can happen:
You are entering a threesome. The odds are that they will most likely bond with each other and you will be left out. Let's face it, why should one spend time with you when there's another of the same kind around?
If the second bird does bond with you, the first bird will feel left out and does start to stress. Budgerigars easily stress out. If you ask a vet about budgie behaviour one question always asked when a budgie is acting differently, is whether there has been a new addition to the family.
So if you want a budgie as companion, one that will bond with you, it is best just to get the one. If you just want listen to their melodious chirping; get more.
Incidentally if you do get another bird it is best to first quarantine the bird for about five weeks before meeting the first bird. Place the second bird in a separate cage and place the cage in a separate room. After the five week period, place them, still in their separate cages in the same room next to each other. Just observe them for a week or so. Provided that no aggressive behaviour is being displayed, it should be safe to introduce them to each other.

Dobbie, an absolutely beautiful Siamese cat resides on one side of the fence and my other neighbour has two tabbies. It originally started with Dobbie walking along the back fence then gaining more confidence to jump down into my back yard, and up onto the kitchen window ledge, peering inside, hoping to catch a glimpse of Limpy. When he couldn't spot him he would just simply jump down and walk away, but when Limpy was seen on the kitchen radio, then he would jump up back on the ledge and spend time just watching him. As long as Limpy stayed within sight that cat didn't budge an inch. The cats seemed to take it in turns watching Limpy.

At first Limpy use to fly away especially if he was startled but he soon got used to them and didn't bother about them. As a matter of fact once he got used to them sitting down on the other side of the window pane he would actually tease them. I couldn't believe it; I wished someone else could see it, to prove me right. Limpy started teasing them by walking back and forth the length of the radio looking directly at them and bobbing his head up and down. The poor cats, all they did was return the stare and drool at the mouth.

Poor Dobbie – he suffered from Limpy incessant teasing

There was many a time I just stood by at a distance observing this interaction. Shaking my head, I told Limpy that if ever they got their paws on him they would not show any mercy. There were times when Limpy would tire of annoying them and fly away either onto my shoulder or back to the bathroom. They would keep on their watch till he was out of sight, before they jumped down and walked away empty handed. On rare occasions they would accept defeat and leave. But there would always be another day and maybe they would get lucky – they never did.

Chapter 5

Every time I left the house I always checked making sure the house was budgerigar safe. Apart from making sure that toilet bowl lids were closed and all windows and outside doors were closed too, I also closed other doors leading to rooms that I did not want Limpy to go to. By now this last action was a waste of time because Limpy followed the same flight paths visiting certain rooms. At no time did he ever deviate, he certainly was set in his ways.

One day as I was about to return a rental DVD, I decided to take Limpy with me in the car. I offered him my finger and placed him on my shoulder, then opened the door that directly leads from the house to the garage. The garage was in darkness and slowly made my way to the car. Sitting there in the darkness Limpy stayed on my shoulder without uttering a single chirp. I looked at him as I pressed the door remote. As it started to roll up, Limpy quickly turned around, still on my shoulder, still without having uttered any sound. I turned the key and as the engine came to life, so did the radio. As soon as it happened he spun around trying to work out where all the noises were coming from. He didn't know which way to look. There was no way I could keep a straight face.

As the car came out into the sunlight Limpy ran from one shoulder to another, madly chirping before turning around and running back again. By the time the car was out in the street, he had swapped shoulders a couple of times. His chirping continued on. As we made our way from one street to another I noticed that he started to spend more time on the right shoulder, which gave him an unobstructed view of the passing scenery. At traffic lights other car travellers noticed the budgie on my shoulder and pointed him out to others. He hopped onto the back of the seat and then flew off to the rear window shelf. There he walked the length of the shelf before once again flying back onto my shoulder. There's no doubt about it he was certainly enjoying this, he hadn't stopped chirping.

A phone call to the agency brought the owner out to collect the DVD. He peeked inside the car looking, searching for the bird. As I passed the DVD through the barely opened window the man whistled, but as expected Limpy wanted no part of him.

Peek-a-boo

Back home I reversed the procedure. In the garage I switched off the engine, closed the garage door, and as soon as the place was in darkness, we got out and entered the house. Limpy briefly looked around, flew off my shoulder for a drink and then took off returning to the bathroom. I walked in and sure enough there he was telling his adventures to the mate in the mirror.

In my daily routine I have a shower after waking up to be followed by shaving and tooth brushing. Limpy was always with me at these times, observing whilst perched on the bathroom radio. Once I have dried myself, he started to fly onto my shoulder and stay there whilst I was shaving. It was here that I noticed that as soon as I switched on the electric razor, Limpy started to chirp and as soon as I switched it off, he immediately stopped. Making sure that I wasn't imagining it I started to test him by switching off the shaver and restarting it a number of times. Sure enough as soon as the shaver sound stopped, he stopped and as soon as it was restarted he too resumed chirping. This test was also conducted using the radio. When it came to the TV he repeated the performance, but only with music clip channels.

I had to laugh, as soon as I switched off the electrical appliance it was like switching off the bird chirping, he instantly stopped. Likewise as soon as I restarted the appliance, Limpy once again gave out a single chirp and a moment later was back in top voice.

As enjoyable as this was there was one major problem. It seemed that Limpy decided to test me out or more importantly tested my patience. I was quite happy to have him on my shoulder whilst watching TV; I was just as happy to hear him merrily chirping away. However, when watching a murder mystery and the police inspector was about to divulge the name of the murderer the last thing I wanted was for Limpy to break out into a song routine. Being momentarily deafened I increased the TV volume only to have Limpy just as effortlessly turn up his volume. By the time I turned around, told him to shut up, which he did, it was too late. The person was named and I missed out. Of course focusing back on the TV again eagerly trying to work out what had happened didn't help, since the chirping had resumed – Aargh

---

A budgie, unless he's sick, will chirp as long as there are other noises around. You can test this by switching off the radio/TV when the bird is chirping and instantly he'll stop. As soon as you start the noise again, he'll start too.

More changes were taking place while carrying out my daily morning bathroom routine. For some reason once I had finished shaving, Limpy flew up on top of my bald head. To some seeing a budgerigar atop a man's head might be considered cute but feeling eight sharp talons as he casually walked about wasn't. Once shaving was over, aftershave lotion is applied. Hardly had I applied the lotion when Limpy, thanks to the rising fumes, started to madly perhaps even uncontrollably, sneeze. What choice did I have, I broke out laughing.

How often one sees a budgie, his head bopping from a miniature version of a hearty sneeze?

Limpy had in the past sneezed; as a matter of fact it is part of his lack of social graces.

He had this incredible timing of sneezing either directly into my glasses, or cheek, or worse, the ear. He must be able to control this for the most inappropriate moment. Picture the following, I had just cleaned my glasses, sat down to watch a movie and as soon as I turned to look at Limpy who had just landed on my shoulder he would do a messy sneeze. There's no "excuse me" or "oh sorry mate". Impeccable timing! So, I got up, cleaned my face and my glasses and sometimes, as soon as I settled down again, it was repeated - aargh.

Mind you on one occasion although not planned I got my revenge. I was sitting down whistling at Limpy who at the time was on my finger. It was a whistling a single short whistle, and then a wait for the reply. He did reply, at his own pace, naturally. Suddenly, without the slightest hint of warning, I sneezed. I didn't even have time to cover my mouth or even turn my head away. It happened so quickly. Limpy was directly in the path taking the full blast of the sneeze. All the feathers were seen to be blown back yet he hardly moved his head at all. I just completely broke down in fits of laughter, because there simply was no expression on his face. It was funnier still when without batting an eyelid he started grooming his feathers, still standing on my finger. It looked as if nothing fazed him.

A few days after he started the sneezing bout Limpy started a new activity. Once I had applied aftershave I filled up a glass of water to rinse after tooth brushing. As I reached for the glass Limpy flew, landed on the rim and had a drink of water. Now that's no big deal, after all a freshly poured water being aerated will always taste better, but this was different. After having had a drink he tried to manoeuvre himself, to squat down, and wet his belly. Over a period of days he did his best but wasn't successful. So, one morning I took in his drinking container and when it was time to rinse my mouth I filled the container. As soon as I presented it to him Limpy flew down, had a drink and then started to manoeuvre himself around stepping in, and squatting down. "Congratulation mate", I cried out, "You're having your first bath". Opening his wings he gently flapped them, moved about and stepping up onto my finger, flew off landing back on my head. Brrr, cold feet mate!

From that day on Limpy never once missed out on his bath. Every morning as I stood still, holding a container filled with cold water, Limpy having gained more confidence merrily splashed about, flapped his wings with more vigour and loudly chirped. He was a sight; again one had to laugh seeing such antics. The unfortunate thing was that when he finished and flew away it was up to me to clean the basin, wall, mirror and tiles from the spilled water. He wasn't doing anything by half. With all his splashing there was hardly any water left in the container, it was all over the bathroom.

It was once again in the bathroom when one morning as I was enjoying a shower and listening to his chirping Limpy suddenly, unexpectedly completely out of the blue whistled, not chirped, but whistled my favourite tune. Instantly I stopped in my tracks and for a moment actually held my breath. Limpy continued chirping. I listened intently hoping upon hope that I did hear correctly, he did whistle. I waited and waited, I was so sure that he had whistled but unfortunately I began to believe that I must have imagined it.

I finished my shower, shaved, and after his daily bath continued on. I looked at him so many times as if I was willing him to whistle but all he did was chirp. Disappointed I walked out, fetched some fresh clothes and sat down on the bed. Limpy as usual would fly over and walk around me as I dressed. As I was putting on a T shirt I heard Limpy whistle. There was no doubt this time, he was near my ear and the sound was unmistakeable. I turned to look at him and whistled back. He looked over and again whistled. I was overjoyed, he looked at me, tilted his head as if to say "what's the big deal?" Although all he had done was to mimic my whistle, to me it was a big deal.

I had another pleasant surprise when two days later not only did he whistle my favourite tune but suddenly whistled another tune. This was so unexpectedly that I looked around as if to find someone else to ask whether I had heard correctly. Sure enough Limpy actually whistled both tunes and lengthened the duration. From then on there was no holding him back; Limpy balanced his chirping with the whistling.

Just over six months had now passed since Limpy came into my life and it has been one educational, entertaining and hilarious adventure.

And laughter was never far away. One morning I was doing the washing up. Limpy was on the radio walking over the dials and knobs and switches. Once he reached the end, turned around, and walked back to the other end. I wished I knew what he was thinking, as he paraded by, all the while letting out a chirp or two. It clearly showed that he was enjoying himself.

I was busy watching him whilst my hands where under soapy water washing the dishes. At one particular moment, and keep in mind that it happened so fast, Limpy either tripped on one of the dials/switches/knobs or simply missed his footing, either way he fell off the radio falling straight down into the sink. As luck would have it, he landed on a plate that I was, at that precise moment bringing up to the surface being now covered in soapy water. The silence was broken by his full throttled shriek.

If you were anywhere in the kitchen you would have looked up just in time to hear Limpy shrieking but just as important to see him take off with a trail of soap suds following, like some exotic birds' tail. Limpy was in an absolutely foul mood, gaining height as he madly flapped his partially wet wings. I wasn't in any position to help. By this time I had dropped the plate as I doubled over in laughter. I was surprised that it didn't shatter when it hit the faucet.

Looking at Limpy through tear strained eyes I fell over laughing as Limpy perched up on top of the kitchen cupboards and started cleaning/grooming with soap suds still piled on his head. It looked like he was wearing a white hat. That created more laughter. It took a good 15 minutes before Limpy stopped preening and I stopped laughing.

Chapter 6

I stated that life with Limpy was one educational, entertaining and a hilarious adventure. But the following month my life changed and Limpy showed a different side of his nature.

One Monday evening while I was at work I was involved in a rather horrific industrial accident. A four ton steel plate peeled off a magnetic crane and hit my left leg shattering the bone and crushing the leg. I was rushed to the Alfred hospital. The following day I was operated on and ten days later I gladly was discharged. All I wanted to do was to return home and try to rebuild my life. Gone were a number of activities that I use to enjoy. Thankfully seeing my winged mate was one activity that I could still participate in. In my absence my brother had looked after Limpy, daily changing his food and water.

Grateful to return back home I spotted Limpy on my bed. As I approached him I was shocked at his condition. He looked a complete wreck; I couldn't help mumble "Oh my God what happened to you?" Gone was the streamlined look. His feathers seemed to have lost all their colours and shine. They looked all matted. He looked like a leper. On crutches I hobbled closer and presented my finger for him to step on to. For the first time ever, Limpy backed away; he literally took a couple of steps back, then flew away, landing on the curtain rod.

I needed to sit down so I too backed away, hobbled back into the lounge room reasoning that since I have been away, he most likely was stressed out, so I needed to give him time to get used to me again.

I sat down on the lounge chair, switched on the TV and for the umpteenth time relived the accident. I didn't pay much attention to the TV and started to wonder what the future held. In that detached behaviour I didn't notice Limpy flyby.

The tapping sound of his beak on the feed container was what brought me back to reality. I watched him eat, his head bopping as he rapidly picked up each seed, crack it open eat it and repeat the process once again.

Of course one should never pat a budgerigar. There's a mistake made by some owners of patting their budgies – DON'T. Do not pat your budgie. He's not a dog. Dogs love to be patted. A dog irrespective of its size is able to absorb patting action onto his body regardless whether it is a soft or hard pat. A bird on the other hand because of its size isn't able to. Yes I know that you will be gentle but a slight change in the hand position will make a difference. The slightest increase in patting with the finger can be harder than anticipated. Observe two budgies, they do not pat themselves they caress each other - do the same.

After he had finished his snack and had a drink he flew over straight onto my shoulder. He would never know how grateful I was to him for that action. I felt so lonely sitting down looking at my damaged leg propped up on the stool and a row of medicine bottles at my fingertips. This time as he sat on my shoulder, something that he has done so many times in the past, felt special. I turned to look at him, whistled and was pleasantly surprised that he returned the look and chirped. I would have loved to have patted him, just like one would a dog.

Isn't it typical, that just as I finally found a comfortable position where the leg pain was at a minimum, the phone rang! A cordless phone is the first item on the must have list. I awkwardly got up and hobbled to the phone, with Limpy doing his best to balance on my shoulder.

My first day back home seemed to pass so slowly and I was looking forward to go and lie down. The surprise was that when I finally did sit down on the bed Limpy was still on my shoulder. The only time that Limpy did move off me was to eat and drink.

Slowly, well let's face it with a crushed leg I wasn't going to move fast, I eased myself down onto the bed. I turned onto my right side so that the right leg could support the injured one. I assumed that Limpy would fly but instead he moved and took up position on my upper left arm. And there once the bedside lamp was switched off stayed till morning. When I woke up I was surprised to realize that I had slept so soundly and then to see him busily grooming himself, still in the same spot.

Again apart from when I was showering and when he was eating or drinking, Limpy stayed on my shoulder all day long and for the next three days. I couldn't go anywhere without him being present. He wasn't going to let me out of his sight. On one occasion I stood up and hobbled to the bathroom while he was eating. As soon as I moved out of view I could hear the unmistakeable beat of the wings as he flew over and back onto my shoulder. On the third day the phone rang and he flew over onto my shoulder as I got up to answer it. From that day onwards every time the phone rang it was a race to see who could reach it first.

On the fourth day as soon as I woke up before I even opened my eyes, I felt that he wasn't on my upper forearm. Afraid of even moving, I opened my eyes to see Limpy directly in front of my face asleep, hutched up on the pillow. I blinked, but more in disbelief. Slowly and holding my breath for fear of disturbing him, I moved my head back to get a better view. I don't believe this? How do I explain this to anyone? Where's the camera when you need it? Moving my eyes around the room as if I could find an answer I once again looked at this sleeping bird.

I had to get up, I had to take my morning medication yet I did not wish to disturb him. What would I do? Focusing ahead I looked at the bedside clock radio. Glad to know that it was still too early for the medication I closed my eyes started to breathe easily once again, and let sleep envelope me.

When I woke up again Limpy wasn't to be seen. But I could easily hear him; he was having a rather heated discussion with his bathroom mirror mate. Probably explaining why he hasn't been around?

Painfully I raised myself off the bed into a sitting position; the left leg was throbbing in pain, but the ears enjoying listening to a healthy budgie, merrily chirping in the bathroom.

This industrial accident had changed me. Unable to walk without the aid of crutches, and wholly dependent on opioid medication to control the pain, I slowly watched time go by. The television and the computer to a degree helped pass the time but for an outdoor person I became a prisoner in my own house. A certain level of depression set in. Is it possible for a bird to sense a change in a human? Limpy had changed too, and he began to spend more time on my shoulder. There were moments when I couldn't go to the bathroom without him following.

Spending more time on my shoulder was one thing but what followed a couple of days later was something so rare, so totally unexpectedly that even now, years later, a listener finds it so hard to accept, that questions are raised.

One morning I woke up hearing the sound of wings flapping and Limpy landing on my prone body. I opened my eyes just in time to see Limpy walking on my stomach towards my head. Although quite curious to see what he was up to, I quickly closed my eyes shut. I felt him walking all the way to the sheets edge and then he jumped onto my chin. He wasn't exactly fussed where he placed his feet. Feeling a talon enter a nostril just about brought a tear to my eyes. Squeezing my eyes shut he walked all the way to my forehead. There he spun around, I felt him lean forward and softly, very softly let out the whistle I usual use to call him with. Perfect in pitch, the whistle was barely audible. I wanted to hear it again, so I didn't move a muscle. Sure enough a moment later Limpy let out the same tune.

He's actually waking me up I thought, I like this; I'll sit still and wait for the whistle again. Yes, he whistled again except this time as loudly as possible, loud enough to be heard from across the street. Hearing such a shrill from only a few inches away sent my ears ringing. Clearly Limpy hadn't been blessed with unlimited patience. I promised myself that in future I would respond on the first wake up call.

The following morning the scene was repeated. Limpy landed on my chest, walked all the way to my forehead, spun around and in the softest of whistling, broadcasted the wakeup call. Oh yes, I learned my lesson, as soon as he finished, I whistled back.

There were times that as soon as I felt him land on the bed I would open my eyes just enough to see him. I could see him walking over the folds in the sheeting, one minute visible next moment down between the folds. He looked determined, slowly walking over, sometimes stumbling, but never quitting. Why didn't he just land on my forehead instead, I'll never know. It wasn't easy keeping a straight face.

Once he woke me up he would briefly stay on me, perhaps to catch his breath before taking off, most likely going to say g'day to his mate in the mirror.

Rarely had he ever missed this performance.

On Tuesday and Thursday mornings I reported to physiotherapy and by the time I returned back home I was mentally, and especially physically exhausted. An afternoon requirement was a short nap. Quite often when I dozed off on the lounge chair I felt Limpy on me either softly chirping or simply just staying on my shoulder. This wasn't the behaviour for such a little bird; this was the loyalty of a faithful friend.

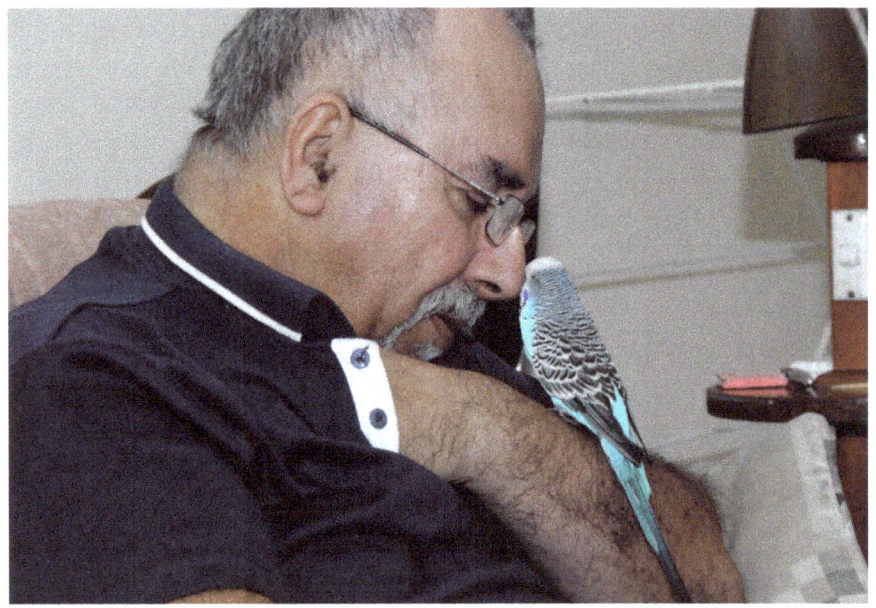

My mate!

He certainly made life a bit more bearable being as I was, stuck at home.

One day while observing him looking at his reflection in the bedroom mirror, I thought back to the day I first picked him up. How fortunate I was to have this budgerigar. I remembered that when I arrived at Tony's place he was gently scratching the area behind his head. I decided that the time had come for me to try and scratch Limpy's head.

I approached Limpy with a finger extended, ready to try and scratch his head. The problem was that as soon as he saw the finger he would instantly jump on. This proved to be a hindrance. There was no point in moving the finger from behind because his natural instinct would be to fly away. So I started to caress his wings, ever so gently, I would run the back of my finger along the outside of the wing and then repeat the performance on the other wing. It wasn't easy because as soon as I deviated he would either jump on, or take off. It took just over a week before he would stand still long enough and let me caress him in such a manner. Slowly I started to move my finger towards the back of the head. I knew when I had reached the right spot, Limpy let out a single chirp that was just barely audible. There was no doubt he loved this. I started to gently move my finger back and forth. Unfortunately I couldn't do it for very long due to the strain on the finger from moving it as lightly and as delicately as possible. As soon as I withdrew my finger Limpy turned around and looked at me. I just broke up laughing.

From that moment onwards head scratching became a daily routine. Limpy thoroughly loved it. As soon as I start he'll lower his head, lower his body as if he was sitting down and start softly chirping. A minute or two later he would partially close his eyes. If he could talk, I'm sure he would say that this is better than sex.

I enjoyed scratching the back of his head however sooner or later I had to eventually stop. As soon as I pulled my hand away he would stand up, move towards my hand, turn his head and present his neck again. Telling him that my finger was tired wasn't an option.

Scratching Duties 1

Scratching Duties 2

One day shortly after we started this daily routine, by accident I flexed my right hand thumb while Limpy was on my knee. I don't know how or what or why but he must have perceived that, that was some sort of a signal, because he walked over and used my thumb as a scratching post. I was so surprised by this action that I filmed it.

You can see this clip on YouTube - http://www.youtube.com/watch?v=npjnHBQtaKA.

Meanwhile physiotherapy exercises were starting to take effect and when the medication was at its maximum strength I was able to move about much more confidently. I 'tested' myself one very early morning when I was woken up by Limpy madly flying about in the bathroom. Limpy had a night terror. Similar to a human having a nightmare, a bird night terror causes the bird to fly about aimlessly. Grabbing my crutches I hopped over urgently reaching out for the light switch. Limpy was struggling, flapping his wings

Start scratching the back of a budgie's head is one action that budgies positively love. This scratching action helps calm the bird. The more you do it the more he will like it and don't be surprised if in time he seeks your finger out to do more scratching action. This in turn helps the bonding between the bird and the owner.

on the floor behind the toilet bowl. I quickly picked him up and held him against my bare chest. Holding him close to my bare chest helped him to slowly calm down, as he felt secured in my hands, plus feeling my body warmth. I softly spoke to him repeated any familiar words such as 'hello' or 'g'day' I whistled favourite tunes, anything that he had heard countless times. In time he settled down. I filled his drinking container with fresh cold water and offered it to him. He greedily drank some.

Leaving the light on, I went back to my bed placing Limpy on my upper arm. A few minutes after I laid down he whistled and briefly chirped. I returned the whistles. I had left the bathroom light on but now switched off the bedside light. We exchanged whistles again than silence. I dozed off. At dawn he woke me up as he usually does. I returned his whistle. He continued to whistle and I continued to respond as it is normally expected. He flew off, went back to the bathroom and I could hear him chirping with his mate in the mirror. I got up, switched off the light, turned over and went back to sleep.

I was most interested to see how Limpy would behave with other people staying at my place. When I had visitors he would go and spend more time in the bathroom away from them. A few hours later once they departed he would return back to me. But one day friends from New South Wales who were passing through were going to spend a few days here in Sunny Melbourne. Well that morning it wasn't sunny, it was positively bucketing down. As I was having the usual morning cuppa I was looking out the window watching it pour. I pointed out to Limpy who was on my shoulder that he was lucky being with me inside rather than out there in that deluge. He looked at me and seeing that I had finished breakfast took off - that's gratitude

---

A bird might experiences a night terror when something or someone passes an uncovered cage. It can also be a shadow from a window that causes the bird to panic and instantly try to take flight. If that happens to your bird the first thing to do is to light up the area. Switch on as many lights, flood the area. The lights must be as bright as possible; this will help him see that everything is normal. A soft light can and will throw shadows again, and that is the last thing a bird wants to see. Holding and letting him feel warmth is best. Don't forget to softly talk or whistle anything that he has often heard before. It takes time for the bird to return back to normal. If the bird lives in a cage do not completely cover it.

for you. He's buddy – buddy when there's food around but once it is gone, so is he.

An hour or so later Alan and Marie arrived. As soon as they showed up they just managed to see him as he did a high speed dash to the bathroom. I doubt whether he was going to come out. Talking and laughing over coffee was the order of the day. Eventually, Limpy came out flying at maximum height and top speed back into the kitchen for a snack. Half way through his meal I excused myself and started to walk out of the room, Limpy immediately took off scattering seeds everywhere and landed on my shoulder. They said that they have never seen a budgie follow the owner. They pointed out that their dog doesn't act as such and envy me for having such a loyal bird. I laughed, I said that at times I can't go anywhere, including going to the toilet, without him following.

In the afternoon my leg started to ache so I excused myself and went to lie down for a while. Practically all this time Limpy had been either on the kitchen radio or my shoulder. Once again as soon as I got off the lounge chair and started making my way to the bedroom Limpy flew over straight onto my shoulder and stayed there. I lay down in bed, slowly turned over onto my right side and Limpy maneuvered himself from my shoulder onto my upper arm. When I woke up Limpy was asleep on my arm. I slowly moved my arm, he woke up, stretched his wings and as I sat up in bed he climbed back up onto my shoulder. When I entered the lounge room they once again commented about having such a loyal bird. Marie approached Limpy but he wanted no part of her at all, not the slightest interest. As soon as she came close he moved hiding behind my neck. She broke up laughing when she saw him peaking around my neck to see if she was still there.

On Sunday morning we woke up quite early for a quick breakfast before my friends departed to catch the ship to Tasmania. Limpy was quite confused seeing so much activity so early in the morning. Before saying goodbye Marie once again with finger outstretched, approached Limpy. Cautiously he did step on her finger, but within a few seconds, took off, once again flying over and hiding behind my neck.

As soon as they departed and silence once again descended, life in "Limpy's household" returned to normal. He flew about visiting all his mirror mates. He was once again back in his domain.

Unfortunately that wasn't the case with me. I thought I was doing well having mastered the use of crutches. However nine months after my industrial accident leg x-rays showed that the first operation wasn't a success and I had to go back to hospital for another operation. Great, that means that apart from more pain I had to start physiotherapy from the start, all over again.

Chapter 7

While I was away I had left the hallway light and the kitchen radio switched on so that Limpy would not feel abandoned. Every second day my brother or nephew would come in and change his food and water. Thirteen days later I showed up, this time propped up with a new set of crutches. Limpy would never know the joy I felt when once again struggling with the two front door steps I hopped into the hallway in time to hear his chirping. It was so good to see him. I whistled 'our tune' and a moment later all I saw was a blur of blue and one long loud chirp as he flew straight towards me.

A few weeks before I entered hospital I noticed that sometimes, when the mood strikes him, Limpy would produce a burst of high speed as he approached the kitchen, when banking right after crossing the hallway, out of the bedroom; it was very much like he was showing off his flying. This was the case here. In an instant he was right in front of me using my chest to halt his progress. Using his beak and both feet he clawed his way up to my shoulder. This was the first time that both my brother and nephew saw the strong bond between us.

I don't know how Limpy did it, how does he work out the time period, but once again for the next four days and three nights he stayed on me, except when it was time for him to eat or during my daily shower.

I hated this, once again sitting down in front of the TV with the left leg propped up. A few more months of physiotherapy, pain, medication, and just watching the world go by.

A change of postman brought a pleasant surprise. The new postman had years earlier spent time on crutches due to a road accident and knew the difficulty of getting about. He suggested, and I quickly agreed, that if I had any mail he would knock on the window, I would then open the garage door with the remote, and he would literally deliver my mail directly into my hand. Sure enough two days later a knock on the window, a garage door opened and more bills pressed into my hands.

My neighbour Marian was also a welcomed visitor and I gratefully accepted her help in carrying out my shopping. Meanwhile Limpy who by now had other humans whistling at him was still trying to work out who these strangers were. No fingers at attention caused him to fly to them. He either took off heading towards the bathroom loudly protesting their presence, or seeking protection, quickly hid behind my neck.

One morning my neighbour George from the house opposite completely surprised me by walking straight into my house. Looking at my stunned expression he pointed out that my garage door was open. Checking for myself, I discovered that indeed it was opened. I wondered how long it had been like that. Surely, it hadn't been opened all night. The same incident happened again three days later except this time it was the postman who said that I must have seen him coming, yet wondered how I knew he had mail for me. Again I was lost for words trying to figure out what was going on.

All was revealed later that day when I heard the door opening. Hobbling into the lounge room, I arrived just in time to see Limpy pressing the button on the remote. Oh for goodness sake, that's all I want now, a budgie who's into electronics. Before I had time to close the door he once again had stepped on the button and did the deed himself. From that moment on the remote was relocated elsewhere.

Apart from my neighbours and the postman, other visitors did on occasions showed up to say g'day. I seriously thought about placing signs on the outside doors informing the visitors to keep the doors closed. I didn't practice what I preached though because the only culprit, who did leave a door open, apart from my brother, was me.

It isn't easy to run whilst on crutches, a fast hobble is an invitation to a fall and that's the last thing I wanted to experience. But when I saw Limpy looking at me across an open door, I just about jumped out of my skin with fright.

Although I had home help I felt uncomfortable to have someone do the laundry. When I ran out of my underwear I worked out a plan to do my washing. Once the clothes were put on the line I returned back to the garage where the washing machine was, and drained it. As soon as I entered the garage I saw Limpy looking directly at me while perched on a kitchen chair. Somehow I had left the door which leads from the house to the garage open. As I said I just about jumped out of my skin with fright. Here was Limpy merrily chirping in the house looking at me outside with the door wide open.

Believe me; I very quickly closed the garage door and then the door leading into the house. Once I drained and put the washing machine away, I opened the door and Limpy was still there chirping and whistling with his eyes directly on me following my every move.

Once I brought in the clothes off the line and folded and put them away, I made up the bed. Now that is an interesting exercise in its own right, supporting myself on crutches it seemed to take forever. In the meantime Limpy was on top of the bedroom curtain rod looking down at me whilst chirping and whistling. What are you mate, a supervisor? You would think that he could give me a helping hand!!

> If ever a bird flies out of a house it would have been useless to call him back. The odds of actually returning back are rare. A person has the ability to return back home because, by using reference points, is able to work out where he is. A bird on the other hand isn't able to reason the same way. Once the bird takes off its aim is just watching where it's heading and not looking around. The bird doesn't take any reference points to be able to retrace its flight.

"Oh I see" my brother cried out, "it is OK to fly and land on me when I come in and replace the food but now that Frank's back you don't want to know me" We all laughed as once again Limpy was shying away from my brother, landed on my shoulder and walked behind my neck. I told the family about the previous day shock when I saw Limpy looking at me through the outside door. It was suggested that if I trimmed his flight feathers that wouldn't be a problem. I reeled back in horror saying that I was completely against that idea. I find it a cruel thing to do to any bird.

Living with Limpy

Wing clipping debate can be quite a sensitive topic. The manager of the local pet shop agreed with me. He pointed out that close to 80% of people request to have the flight feathers clipped when buying a budgerigar. I said that I abhor the practice. He agreed, but then also said that not everyone has a Limpy.

There's an argument that a bird outside the cage can fly out of the house or try and fly into a window pane. My reply is why the bird should suffer because the owner fails to close the front or back door. As for the window, just lower the blinds till the bird get used to the fact that he can't fly through does work.

Parents with a little foresight and planning can make a house as safe as possible for a toddler. If this is so easily achieved why not the same adjustment made for a bird, why cripple him. If you want a bird to fly around the house simply make the house safe for him. Closing the toilet lids is the first priority. Make sure that the windows are closed or just ajar. The same can be said for the outside doors, keep them closed. If the owner does want to leave the door open to let fresh air in than install a fly wire screen or the placing of plastic strips where a person can go in or out but a bird will never fly through. You can see these strips at restaurants or any establishment that does not want to let flies in.

I was asked how one does prevent a bird from landing on curtain rods as this results in the curtains being stained from the droppings? There's a very simple step to follow – roll two sheets of paper and place against the wall and along the rod. They don't stick out, they're practically invisible. Budgies do not like landing on a soft surface because the surface isn't stable. As soon as they feel it giving way they'll take off again.

Finally keep in mind that wing clipping is quite stressful to a bird. Cutting flight feathers is to suit the owner not the bird.

Chapter 8

As the days turned into weeks, the time slowly passed watching TV or being on the computer. Crippling pain and wholly relying on crutches I lived in the lounge room. At times the house felt like prison. The only time I went out was to physiotherapy.

Is it possible that in these depressing surroundings Limpy felt the pain I was going through? When you think about it what would a bird, such a tiny bird know about human emotions? He seemed to once again spend so much time with me on my shoulder. Mind you, I wasn't complaining, his antics were hilarious.

Although I was on very strong pain killing medication, I always looked forward to sleep, because in that state there is no pain. Waking up brought pain, but it also brought the daily wakeup call from Limpy.

One morning, Easter Sunday to be precise; as per usual Limpy flew over landing on my stomach and once again started the arduous walk all the way to my face. Once there he walked over my mouth and nose, he didn't care what he stepped on, and arriving on my forehead, turned around and started his daily wakeup call duties. After replying by whistling back he stayed on my forehead. I briefly opened my eyes and shut them again in case he started to walk back down. He didn't, being bald headed doesn't help Limpy to hold on to anything and on this particular morning, Limpy lost his footing, slipped and landed onto my shoulder/pillow and then tumbled down finally landing between the pillow and my body. A rather loud shrill announced his displeasure. I looked down and broke up laughing. A moment later he ruffled his feathers and started to walk under the raised covers towards my feet. Where are you going I asked? As I continued to raise the covers he continued walking further towards my feet. I didn't believe it.

"Oi," I called out, "it's a bit too early to go underground exploring". Limpy didn't listen. Slightly lowering the covers and reducing the light, soon saw him race back up towards the pillow. I rolled over, presented my finger and he stepped up. Now unhindered by the clothing surrounding him he took off, headed straight to the bedroom mirror and, I assume, report his findings to his mate.

Honestly, Limpy must have thought that he owned this castle and had the right to do whatever he wanted.

Spending the days stuck at home, visitors were always welcomed. Those who often came around got used to seeing Limpy. They often asked me to relate his latest adventure. The word 'character' was often used to describe him. Apart from the bathroom mirror I installed another in the bedroom and two small hand held ones in the kitchen, one on the counter and one on top of the fridge.

Over time Limpy started displaying different behaviour in front of them. His actions in front of the mirror on top of the refrigerator were definitely different from all the behaviour in front of the other three. When I introduced him to this mirror Limpy would approach it and started to chirp and gently touch the mirror with his beak. At times the chirping was loud, other times at a more accepted level. But that changed.

Someone has to annoy the bird inside this thing

Just keeping you company, mate.

Limpy would slowly almost cautiously walk up to it, peck it, and then run away to the edge of the fridge. It was as if he was trying to annoy that bird and then run away before he was caught out. He would do this a number of times. Then for reasons known only to him, he would again walk towards the mirror but this time go to the edge and 'peak' around as if to see the bird from the back. A moment later he would return to the edge of the fridge and eventually take off. He then without fail flew to the bathroom and 'reports' his activity to that mate. It was one of the strangest acts that I had ever seen him carry out. This was repeated almost every day.

He was quite happy to just sit next to his reflection against the mirror on the kitchen counter. No chirping or whistling, no beak touching, just silently looking in or standing by.

Soft chirping or making faces and moving along the frame were the order of the day at the bathroom mirror. Without fail the bedroom mirror was there to argue with. Loud, boisterous screeching, taking off, turning around and landing once more on the frame and repeat the screeching. That mirror was made for arguing. I wished I knew what was said. Taking a guess I could well imagine Limpy saying "don't just sit there say something"

Visitors laughed when I told them of his different behaviour leading them to state that it looked like Limpy had a separate personality for every mirror.

Another unusual behavior surfaced again when on one occasion I had to go to physiotherapy. For some reason while I was dressing which wasn't easy when the left leg was strapped out and unable to be bent, Limpy was all over me. Try putting on a sock while a bird hangs on to it, to be followed by putting on a T shirt while he's on the shoulder and doesn't want to move.

Before I had breakfast I changed his water and seeds but he continued to stay on me. Breakfast was consumed, while he either walked up and down my arm or stayed on my shoulder and stretched out to groom my nose. A moment later he would walk down and start grooming my thumb. This continued on throughout breakfast and even when clearing the table and doing the washing up. I wouldn't say it was strange, but unusual. Whatever I did he stayed on me. I would love to know why, why is he behaving like this? It looked like he didn't want me out of his sights. I remember what my next door neighbour said - he truly is a one off. Waiting for the right time I sat down with a book. Limpy would fly off after I had been sitting still for about five minutes. At the appropriate time, I walked around the house and made sure it was 'budgie safe' before departing for my medical appointment. Limpy was eating just as I opened the door leading to the garage. He instantly stopped eating and looked at me. He just remained motionless, not moving a muscle. I remembered my mobile phone, walked back to fetch it and walked back to the door. Other than turning his head to follow my movement, he was still. I said "see you" as I closed the door. As soon as I was out of sight he called out my 'hello' whistle. Three more times he called out, and then stopped. Honestly I just stood still in a dark garage wondering what he was thinking about, what he could be doing now. Curiosity overtook me and I opened the door and looked in. As soon as he saw me he flew straight over landing on my head. Well I couldn't go out like that.

I walked back into the kitchen and leaned over the counter, motionless. It was a good four minutes before he took off and went back to his feeding. I hurriedly left, walked out, closing the door behind me. He again called out my 'hello' whistle to be followed with a rather half-hearted one and then silence. This time I walked away, got into the car and drove out.

As I started the car I thought of a parent who is trying to sneak out but was spotted by a toddler who started to cry. You want to stay but have no choice, and sadly leave. I really would love to know what he was thinking all that time.

That wasn't the first time that Limpy seemed to behave like a child. This was clearly demonstrated one stormy night. I was comfortable sitting down in the lounge chair watching TV while lightning and thunder was raging outside. A movement to my right caught my attention and as I looked in that direction, I saw Limpy come flying out of the darkened room at full speed heading straight towards me. I didn't even have time to react. He landed on my left arm and practically ran up to my shoulder and hid behind my neck. He startled me, I certainly wasn't expecting him. I put the ice cream bowl on the coffee table and reached out for him. He avoided my finger and moved out of reach. He was determined to stay at the back of the neck. I got up, closed the curtains and switched on the lounge room lights. I walked and switched on the dining and hallway, flooding the whole area with light. It took sometime before he walked out from behind my neck to the shoulder and jumped on my finger as soon as I moved it into position.

He was still pacing and you could see his heavy breathing. I started to talk, very softly, telling him that "everything is OK" "there's nothing to worry about" and "you're safe". In time I could see that he was calming down. Forty minutes later, although still raining, the lightning show had abated. Limpy, being Limpy thought of his stomach; flew off and after a snack and a drink flew over.

I had once again turned my attention to the TV. He flew towards the bathroom but returned due to the darkness. Limpy was able to fly from a dark to a lit room, but not the other way around. I got up and lit up the bedroom and bathroom. A moment later he flew back to the bathroom landing on the towel rack. I switched off the bathroom light but had learned to leave the bedroom light on. If I had switched it off he would have come out again.

About fifteen or so minutes later I peeked in; I could see that he was fast asleep so I flicked the bedroom light off and silence once again descended on the house.

The following night there was another commotion. Limpy woke me up when I heard urgent wing flapping. Limpy was having a night terror. I jumped out of bed, rushed into the bathroom switching on every light I could find. Limpy was on the floor and as soon as the lights came on he flew to me. Once again I spoke softly, whistled familiar tunes and said familiar words. Once his breathing slowed down back to normal I went into the kitchen and returned with his water container; it looked like he gulped down a lot of drops. He flew back to the towel rack. A quarter of an hour later I switched off the lights, turned in and just listened for any sounds, normal or otherwise.

When Limpy woke me up I was curious to see how he behaved, would the fright a few hours ago cause him to react or behave in a different way. Maybe it was my imagination but he didn't seem to be as active as usual. After breakfast I decided to keep an eye on him.

As I had to finish a task on the computer I took him with me to my study. The study wasn't Limpy's favourite room. Unless he was on the back of the chair before jumping onto my shoulder, which could sometimes startle me, he was either walking on the desk directly in front of me or jumping onto the keyboard.

Paperwork – it never ends

Living with Limpy

This particular morning I was so busy working on the computer that I didn't realise that he wasn't around. It was then that I noticed how quiet the house was. Usually I would hear Limpy flying or whistling and chirping or having an argument with his mate in the mirror. This was not the case; the house was as quiet as an undiscovered tomb.

I stood up and went looking for him. I couldn't find him, I checked every little known area where he hung out, but I couldn't see him anywhere. I knew that he couldn't fly away because all three outside doors were closed. I whistled but no response. It's called selective deafness. I checked the bathroom, bedroom and lounge room, still no sign anywhere. I walked into the kitchen and checked the top of the fridge and the window sill radio; again he was nowhere to be seen. Where was he hiding, I bet you, he's up to something.

It was then in the kitchen that I heard a very soft chirp. Turning around I just managed to catch a glimpse of his head.

I'm going to shoot that bird. He isn't a budgie, he's a flying misfit. I made the mistake of not closing the pantry door. There at eye level Limpy had flown in and landed in the 5 litre plastic container that was full of his seeds. He had crouched down on top of the seeds and was casually, at his own pace helping himself to a seed now and then. As I approached him I could see that he had his eyes half closed - well mate, don't let me stop you, make yourself at home. As soon as he saw me he flew over onto my shoulder and I saw three shelves being liberally sprayed with spilled seeds. I turned my head towards him as if to say 'thanks', he looked at me, chirped twice and crouched down on my shoulder for a nap. – Aargh

I was wrong, he was back to normal.

As you can well imagine moving about on crutches isn't exactly graceful and showering can be an adventure in just balancing. Quite often when I had a shower Limpy stayed on the shower screen frame looking down at me.

One morning his timing was off. At the moment of closing my eyes and lathering my head Limpy came in on full throttle and tried to land on it. It was definitely not his best landing because he ricocheted off. Feeling him hitting my shoulder and knee before landing between my wet feet, it wasn't hard to figure out what had happened. All I heard was flap, flap and then splat.

I dared not move for fear of stepping on him. I quickly washed my face and then cautiously bent down, reached out and picked him up. Covered in soap he was slippery and I was apprehensive on how tight to hold him. He was soaked to the skin. He looked as if he was wearing a drooping moustache. I just lost the plot and burst out laughing. Limpy looked positively miserable. Reaching up I gently placed him on top of the shower screen frame and continued with my shower. Next second as he unsuccessfully tried to take off I felt him hit my shoulder and down he went near my feet for the second time. This time the splat was louder. I was very concerned that he had hurt himself. Once again I picked him up but now I held him and very quickly rinsed off.

Try walking out of a shower stall, while holding a soap covered bird in one hand and a crutch in the other on a wet floor. This time I placed him on the towel rack only to see him once again try to fly. The resulting fall saw him land on the bathroom floor, mercifully without any harm. He loudly screeched and walked away in disgust. By the time I retrieved my crutches he had run away to the bedroom and out into the hallway. Picture a limping, naked, wet human chasing an equally limping naked wet bird - a comedy in action! Picking him up off the floor wasn't easy either. I hurriedly dried myself and then started to dry him too. I quickly put on a T shirt and placed him on my shoulder. He moved and positioned himself directly behind my neck. He stayed put, didn't move at all till I sat down for breakfast.

Spotting a slice of vegemite toast saw him walk down and stop directly in front of the plate. His wings might be temporarily out of action but his taste buds were still in proper working order. Once he consumed his portion of toast he turned around and momentarily looked at me. With a curious look I followed his progress as he gingerly walked down my arm than hopped onto my stomach, jumped onto my knee cap and then hesitantly took off and gently landed on the floor. Sensing that he once again had found his wings, he took off straight towards the bedroom; most likely to report his latest adventure to his mates in the bedroom and bathroom mirrors.

About 30 minutes later Limpy flew out and once again landed on my shoulder. Well one thing was for certain he smelled just like my Palmolive 'Gold' soap – nicely scented. The rest of the day was back to normal, flying about the house, eating, drinking, annoying the neighbour's cat and having whistling/chirping sessions, in short a full rich busy active day.

Chapter 9

It never seemed to amaze me how such a small bird could have so much energy. Throughout the day Limpy was so active, stopping only for food and water. He did take time out for a few minutes of napping but on the whole he got things to do, stories to tell, and songs to sing.

Apart from all this daily activity he also find time hanging around with me or should I say on me, either grooming an ear or nose. He groomed my ear far more often than the nose, but then again it wasn't easy balancing on tip toes to groom the nose. Carrying out the daily chores didn't stop him staying on me doing his best to balance as I moved about.

If you think it is easy to shave while he groomed my ear then think how difficult it is to have him perched on the tooth brush while using it. Apparently that was the best place to keep an eye on me. Mate, you can't get any closer. All I see is a blurred outline of a bird a couple of inches away. I couldn't even brush my teeth in peace – Aargh

Keeping in mind that he's on the go all day long, I was very surprised when while watching a movie a movement caught my eye. I looked towards the bedroom and there was Limpy walking out of the darkened bedroom. I didn't believe it, it's just on midnight; he's supposed to be asleep. Here he was, as casual as can be, walking towards me at a leisurely pace. He crossed the hallway at times looking both ways as if crossing the road. Am I seeing things, this is so out of character I was forced to just sit there with my mouth open, lost for words. Thanks to his limp, he walked in a rather comical penguin style. He entered the lounge room as confidently as a speaker approaching a podium. For some reason known only to him, he stopped, then after surveying the situation flew up onto my knee, ran, and then started climbing over my chest up all the way to my shoulder. He briefly stopped. "Are you catching your breath?" I whispered then he turned around, looked down as if to check his ascent and after a couple of chirps, obviously he wanted to say g'day, flew off to his food and water bowls. I was curious to see what's he was up too that by now I had lost the plot of the movie I was viewing, can you blame me? When he finished he flew over onto my shoulder and just stayed there. No chirping, no whistling, in fact no noise whatsoever, just standing there on my shoulder looking towards the TV. I need someone else to witness this? A budgerigar came out for a midnight snack, and then propped up on a shoulder to watch TV?

When the movie finished I switched off the TV and went to the study. I assumed that he had going back to bed. Nope, no chance, at 1am he started chirping, flying around the study and walking about on the computer keyboard as I was doing my best to type. There was no sign of him slowing down. At 1.30am I switched off the computer and turned in. Even while I was undressing Limpy was still moving about on me. I placed him on the towel rack and as I turned around he was still merrily chirping and whistling. Lying down in bed I switched off the light. Even in the darkness he had to have the last word. After a few more chirps, silence. I smiled, rolled over and went to sleep too.

I wondered where he got his energy from.

If Limpy was with me in my study and decided to go to 'his' bathroom, he never flew straight down the hall into the bedroom and then the bathroom. What he did was go the long way by detouring into the kitchen, then bank left into the dining and lounge room, cross the hallway once again and then enter the bedroom, and finally the bathroom. That was the longest flight he made. This of course resulted in building up his wing muscles to a point where those long flights were done with ease. At times I had noticed his enjoyment of flying, sometimes giving a burst of speed just for the thrill of it.

He firmly believed that, when flying he had right of way. He never deviated from his flight path, I had to duck or get out of his way.

Yes there were a couple of near misses and thankfully only one collision. I had just finished washing the breakfast cutlery. Limpy was doing his morning rounds, visiting his four mirror mates, chirping to one and arguing with another. The kitchen radio had Neil Mitchell chatting to callers and the bedroom radio was playing some old tunes. It was a rather noisy morning. I left the kitchen walking to the bedroom. Just as I turned into the room Limpy was coming out. With so much noise around I did not hear his flapping wings. We were both surprised. I just managed to see him raise his feet up as he started reverse flight. I was able to protect myself by quickly shutting my eyes. A moment later and I felt him collide straight into my nose. Suffering from a blocked nostril is one thing, having a few sharp talons invade said nostril didn't help at all. It was enough to make my eyes water.

Limpy fell, but managed to fly out, before reaching the ground. If you think I was unhappy about the incident you're right but compared to me nursing my nose Limpy's objectionable screeching was far worse. The noises from the radios were nothing compared to the noise he created. Everyone within earshot would have heard Limpy's complaint.

Luck in my view plays a far greater part in life than some are prepared to accept. Occasionally the powers to be, smile, at other times they don't. Here I was sitting down looking at a damaged leg, positive that I would end with a limp yet just a few inches away a wonderful bird with the same left leg limp is peacefully sleeping on my shoulder. The limp certainly hasn't bothered him. I should take a leaf out of his book!

I was overjoyed when I received an invitation to attend a function in Sydney. Just getting out of the house was a treat in itself. If it wasn't for Limpy's presence I would have been climbing the wall. There's a limit to how many TV commercials spliced with a movie, one can view. The four day event meant a change of scenery and catching up with quite a few long lost friends. This was certainly going to be more beneficial than all the medication I was taking.

Marian, my next door neighbour was present when the call came through. Smilingly, she volunteered to look after Limpy while I was away. I was so happy that I had forgotten about Limpy. Eternally grateful for her help I started to make a list of what to take with me. The plan was for her to pop in every morning and replace the water and feed. If it was going to be a hot day she would pop in twice a day and replenish the water. Happy in the knowledge that Limpy would be looked after, I handed Marian my house keys and after telling Limpy to behave got into my car, waved to Marian and headed north towards Sydney.

No four brick walls around me but wide open spaces and a long road stretching out towards the horizon was tonic to my spirit. I felt alive. Time seemed to fly as the minutes turned to hours and then days.

Living with Limpy

On Sunday afternoon, having waved goodbye to my friends and heading south again, I had time to reflect on the event. It was at this time that I realised that I was now missing Limpy. Following a short debate with myself I decided not to stop but drive through the night. I laughed as I suddenly realised I wanted to see him as soon as possible.

In the early hours of the morning my eyes gave me the unmistakeable sign that they wanted to shut down for a while. Yawning didn't help either. Just outside the town of Benalla I pulled over, tilted the seat back and let sleep envelope me.

When I woke up I stepped out embracing the cool early morning chill, limped around to the driver's seat and started the engine. Working out the estimated time of arrival I eased out back onto the road, once again looking forward to returning back home to see Limpy. Marian was surprised when I arrived mid-morning rather than the expected late afternoon. When she asked me what was wrong, why I had driven through the night, I told her that I was missing Limpy.

She smiled, and shaking her head she said that we had truly bonded. "You two are a pair" she chuckled. Although I never thought of it I had to agree when she stated that when that faithful day of days should arrive and Limpy would let me know that the time had come to part, for him to move on, to cross the magical rainbow bridge up in the sky, where food is aplenty and cats are banned, my loss was going to be hard to take. I nodded, she was right.

As soon as I entered the house right there still in the hallway, I whistled 'our tune'. The unmistakeable loud chirping followed by the sound of wings flapping, announced Limpy's arrival. Both Marian and I just broke up laughing. As I said we were in the hallway. Usually I would enter the house straight from the garage and Limpy would cross the hallway, fly past the dining room heading towards the kitchen. This time he did just that except that seeing no one was where he expected, he did a roundabout flight looking for me. He headed straight for me once I was spotted me and landed on my shoulder.

It's a bit hard to say g'day when one is laughing so hard. We made our way to the kitchen and fired up the kettle. Over a cup of coffee Marian told me what happened.

She had spent years trying to get Limpy to jump on her finger without any luck, however by the second day of my absence she once again approached him with her hand outstretched and he jumped on her hand and ran up to her shoulder. She was ecstatic. I'm sure she walked 6 inches off the ground. Now she approached him again but he wanted no part of her. Limpy just walked behind my neck giving her the cold shoulder. Marian shocked her head. "Oh that's nice" she remarked "it's all great mates as long as Frank isn't around, but as soon as Frank shows up, there goes our friendship. Limpy, you certainly know who your true mate is".

As we continued talking and laughing he joined it by merrily chirping away. Due to his racket we actually had to raise our voices which in turn caused him to chirp and whistle louder. Anyone passing by would have sworn there was a party going on.

Shortly after Marian departed, I looked at Limpy eating; yes I said, remembering what Marian said, I certainly will regret the day when he passes away.

Two co-workers were welcomed with open arms when they dropped in for a visit. The electric jug was once again pressed into service. Over a coffee I gladly listened to all the latest gossip. As expected with all the noise we were creating Limpy came flying out into the lounge room landing on my shoulder. Just as one of the lads got up and approached Limpy making whistling noises, it was also clear that the other not only stayed seated but much to my surprise, actually showed an irritation to Limpy's presence. Questions about Limpy were asked and duly answered. The person still sitting down asked the question about the bird's droppings. Although it was a normal question it was the way he asked it that caused me to feel a little annoyed.

I pointed out that my budgie flew around the house, and when not staying on my shoulder, stayed in the kitchen, lounge and bedroom, but mostly in the bathroom, as he slept there. Under his landing zones such as the kitchen and bathroom radio and the towel rack where he sleeps, I had placed a sheet of newspaper. These papers are daily cleaned and replaced on a weekly basis. Following another question, I replied that if I saw any droppings outside the 'established' areas I would just leave until dry and then pick up and dispose of, or use the vacuum cleaner.

Living with Limpy

I was really surprised to see him raise objections about having a pet indoors. I tried to explain that, even if caged, it still required cleaning; the only advantage with letting him fly about the house was more exercise, and the enjoyment of having him in direct contact.

No matter what I said it was quite clear that he objected to an indoor pet, and bitterly complained. Even the other visitor was surprised by this outburst. I told him that I love seeing birds fly especially seeing my budgie in full flight. He wasn't listening, I realised that no discussion was going to change his outlook so I asked him to leave.

Part of owning a bird is to daily inspect his droppings. A normal dropping should be white in the middle and black around the edges. If there's a change such as it being very runny than keep an eye on him. Firstly look at his food dish to see whether he has eaten all the seeds. If there is a small amount of uneaten seeds left that's not a worry but if 50% of the seeds are still untouched than alarm bells should go off. If within a period of time there's no change or he looks worse off, than off to the vet we go. Looking worse means he's hunched over, quiet and lethargic, that's a sign something is seriously wrong. Keep in mind that birds have the ability to disguise the situation. Out in the wild if a bird showed that he was not well, predators would soon become aware and it would lead to a possible attack. Hence they are able to mask their illness.

In my case when it came to Limpy, he was my mate, I am responsible for him. As soon as I saw the first hint or sign of trouble it was a matter of picking him up, placing him in a transport cage, and go straight to a vet.

Chapter 10

In November, on Cup Day 2009 there was no hint of trouble, but when the problem surfaced, it was a sight that I'll never forget.

It was a public holiday so the plan was to sleep in. That was the plan but with Limpy around that was not the case. His policy is that if he's up then everyone should be. Shortly after dawn he, as usual, flew down onto my stomach, walked all the way up to my forehead, and after turning around, looked down and in the softest tone whistled his wake up call. A light breakfast was consumed following the daily routine of shower, shaving and dressing with Limpy all over me. In short a normal day so far.

At lunchtime I went out attending a BBQ held at a friend's place. As usual when I returned back home I called out to Limpy and made my way straight into the bedroom to change. Not hearing the sound of chirping or flapping wings I quickly changed and went looking for him. I became increasingly concerned when I couldn't locate him. I called out a number of times but still no reply. I was relieved to find him walking on the carpet in the study, yet wondered why he was on the floor. In the study, Limpy was either on the computer desk pecking at the calculator or on the back of my chair. I crouched down in front of him.

Relief soon turned to shock

"Stop, don't do that" I cried. "Stop it, what's the matter with you" once again crying out quite loudly. I actually bellowed as if by doing so he would understand. Again I yelled "Stop it." Raising my voice to fever pitch only resulted in gaining a sore throat. Limpy briefly stopped, looked at me and continued the same activity with the same frightening cold indifference.

I looked around as if I could find the answer to the dilemma. There, directly in front of me was my budgerigar biting off his flight feathers. For some unknown reason, this bird which has brought me so much joy was mercilessly, even savagely, tearing his wing feathers apart. Seeing the remains of smaller pieces of feathers behind him, I started to panic. Feeling as if I have been kicked in the stomach, I reached out and gently grabbed him, stopping him from continuing this brutal act. It was easy to catch him. Limpy had caused so much damage to his wings that he couldn't fly away.

I stood up, again looking around for an answer to stop this behaviour. While still holding him, I reached for the phone.

A frantic call to my cousin Tony, who had sold me the bird, soon saw me on the road urgently heading to his place. The usually pleasant thirty minute drive now seemed endless. Every traffic light seemed to turn red holding back my progress, as I reflected back on a three year friendship. What happened in the few hours I was away? What had changed my feathered friend behaviour?

I reflected back on the numerous incidents of the past three years. Do you have any idea how difficult some chores were when one has a budgerigar running up and down one's arm inspecting everything! Try and slowly pour cordial from one bottle to another while he's blocking the view because he has a front seat at the proceedings. He had to be where the action was. Nothing held him back, anything that I did he shared.

Arriving at my cousin's place I gladly surrendered Limpy to him hoping and praying that he had a magical cure. I was shocked that a moment later Limpy bit Tony's wife's finger. This was something totally unexpected; he had never even pecked, let along bit anybody. No it was quite clear; there was something very much wrong with him. Tony inspected him and offered suggestions. He gave me mineral and vitamin powder to add to the water. I gratefully accepted them and shortly after departed. Yet at the back of my mind I couldn't help think that there was a bigger problem than just a lack of vitamins and minerals.

The return trip home was spent planning changes. Limpy couldn't fly so I had to change things around for his benefit. Of the three areas that he liked to sleep in, in the bathroom, the towel rack was the lowest. He had often slept there and it wasn't too high for him to fly down to the ground. Food and drink containers were removed from a table and placed on the lounge room floor near me so as to keep an eye on him. I also placed a notebook and a pen near his food so as to make notes on behaviour.

I completely missed dinner, didn't pay much attention to the TV and when I finally went to bed sleep didn't come easily. As a matter of fact every sound caused me to wake up, worrying about him. Sitting up in bed I could see Limpy on the towel rack. Numerous times I did just that, and kept an eye on him.

"What's wrong with him?" I cried. I searched my mind trying to find anything out of the ordinary that had caused him to behave so destructively. I anxiously tossed and turned all night. It was a disturbed, broken sleep.

I woke up quite early, as a matter of fact, way before him and tip toed out of the bedroom. Walking to the study I saw the damaged feathers from yesterday still bearing silent testimony to what had taken place. I quickly cleaned up and went back into the bedroom. All I did was silently sit on the bed, keeping an eye on him and wondering what else to do if his current behaviour continued. As soon as he started to move I walked into the bathroom and sat on the toilet seat just looking at him. He looked at me, I smiled, I was sure he was thinking that the situation has been reversed. He was supposed to wake me!

After a couple of chirps he walked the length of the towel rack and jumped on my right shoulder then walked around the back of the neck to the left shoulder. As usual I softly whistled and he responded by chirping. The exchange of chirps and whistles went on for a few minutes. We were just enjoying each other's company. Yesterday's incident seemed so far away. Once again he started his daily grooming. A moment later his behaviour changed and I found that the morning brought only despair as once again I saw him literally attack his flight feathers. I once again begged him not to attack them, but I knew my pleas were falling on deaf ears.

It was while showering that I remembered a business card that I had somewhere in my study desk of a knowledgeable bird specialist. Dripping wet I located the card and urgently rang the specialist begging her to see Limpy as soon as possible. Instant dressing, no time for shaving or breakfast, I jumped in the car and with Limpy on my shoulder raced to the Highbury Veterinary Clinic.

The forty minute drive seemed to go on forever, especially when every traffic light once again looked to be working against me. What is this; do they see me coming and turn red? Stationary at traffic lights many a car driver pointed out to their passengers the bird on the driver's shoulder.

I didn't even realise it, I was in such a hurry I walked out to the car and entered the clinic with Limpy still on my shoulder.

Many a question was answered. Dr Patricia Macwhirter, the lady veterinary commented that his wing muscles were very strong, so was his heart, as she listened to it and his weight is perfect. I shuddered however when it was pointed out that she couldn't see what was wrong, therefore only a blood test would explain the birds' behaviour. Recognising his screech out back only increased my stress level. Although he was only out of my sight for a few minutes I was overjoyed to see him again, more so, when she placed him on a table that I was leaning on; he did a high speed run up my arm and onto my shoulder and went directly behind my neck, the spot he favoured when startled or scared.

A liver imbalance was diagnosed as being the cause. She was unable to explain why, but the liver problem plus the heavy moulting was causing Limpy pain, resulting in his attack on his feathers. After typing down some notes she said that I would have to administer three types of medicinal drops into his beak every morning. The first was for pain relief and anti-inflammation. She showed me how to do it and I had to 'practice' doing it in front of her, thus making sure that I understood the procedure.

She gave me strict instructions about the medication stating that no matter how much Limpy screeched and did his best to wiggle out of my hand, I had to be quite strict and administer the medication. Although she wasn't happy with Limpy eating human food she did state that the liver imbalance wasn't due to this. She did however point out that I was not to let him have any more such food. Before I left she removed a number of damaged feathers thus giving new ones the chance to grow.

To administer oral medication it is best to place the budgie in the palm of the hand with the index and middle finger on either side of his head. This will prevent him from turning his head either side. By tilting him slightly backwards it places him in a 'submissive' position and he will recognise this posture which will greatly decrease his struggling. Then it is a matter of just placing the measured dose of medicine in his mouth.

The return trip home was one drive I'll never forget. I kept on picturing holding Limpy the way she showed me how to, and how to administer the medication using a calibrated hypodermic gadget. Briefly catching glimpses of Limpy on my shoulder, he just stood there looking directly ahead. He had 'looked' after me when I returned from hospital, now it was my turn to see him through this crisis. I was momentarily distracted when Limpy walked down my left arm and positioned himself on the steering wheel still looking forward. I didn't believe this; I had to slightly reposition myself and tilt my head to see where I was going because he stood directly in my line of vision. "Pardon me, mate" I briefly chuckled

Back home, in the kitchen as I started to fill his water container Limpy walked down my arm, had a drink and returned back to my shoulder. He was unable to fly; he knew that life had changed. It was obvious he was going to depend on me now more than ever.

From my point of view the change was relatively easy, as he was going to spend more time on the floor all I had to do was to place food and water there and at dusk take him to the bathroom and place him on the towel rack. The only other change was to keep an eye out for him when I walked and administered the medication. Although in the past I have done so I made double sure that if I woke up in the middle of the night I went to the visitor's toilet rather than the on-suite one so as not to disturb him.

From his point, the loss of flight was downright frightening. Limpy tried so hard, so often attempting to fly, madly flapping his wings and running at the same time, all to no avail. He tried again and again till he stopped from sheer exhaustion. I lowered my finger; he jumped on and could see he was breathing quite heavily. I would gladly have given a month's pay for someone to wave a magic wand over him. His landings from either my shoulder or the towel rack weren't exactly perfect, quite often hitting his beak against the carpet. As a precaution I laid out a folded towel on the bathroom floor for a softer landing. I was very worried, wondering how his undercarriage, damaged as it was could take it. I expected a broken leg any day. I examined his walk looking for any change in his limp. At times, after he consumed some food and water I lowered my leg off the stool down to the ground, he hopped on and once I lifted my leg back onto the stool, it was just a matter of him running up my body all the way to the shoulder.

During the day he simply didn't want me to go anywhere unless he was on my shoulder. I quickly learned that I should stay seated if he was eating and drinking. If I moved while he was eating he would instantly run towards me. As soon as I stood up if he wasn't on my shoulder he 'dropped' everything and urgently chirped to pick him up. I learned that certain chirps meant certain signals. If I stood up and walked away from the TV chair he instantly ran behind me, if I managed to go out of sight he ran panic stricken screeching at the top of his voice looking into every open room searching for me. He quickly realised that when I went through a certain door (leading to the garage) I was going to be away for a considerably long time and he cried out using a rather unique double short sharp shrill. It was painful to sit in the car listening to this agonising cry. One day I actually rang and cancelled a medical appointment. When I explained the situation with the receptionist she came up with a plan. I took Limpy with me, stayed in the car and she would wave through the window when it was my turn. I placed Limpy on the back of the seat; got out, saw the doctor to renew my prescription, collected it and back to the car. The appointment lasted no more than 6 or so minutes. Back with Limpy, I then phoned from the car park to book the next appointment.

A single sharp screech signalled his desire to 'turn in' for the night so it was easy to pick him up and take him to the bathroom. When I placed him on the towel rack he screeched as soon as I switched off the lights. Whatever I did he just screeched. More from good luck than good management I switched off the light in the bathroom but left the bedroom light on - no screeching. Fifteen or so minutes later I peeked into the bathroom; he was fast asleep and then switched off the bedroom light.

To prevent stressing out both Limpy and myself, I started to do my shopping late at night. This took place usually an hour or so after I 'put him to bed', because by that time, I knew he would be sound asleep.

We soon settled into a daily routine.

When I had no choice but to go out, upon returning I always found him sitting at the edge of my favourite chair.

Patiently waiting for me

He was able to climb on to the chair by climbing a cloth bag that I had placed leaning against the foot stool. At times I picked him up; other times whistled and made my way to the bedroom to change. He always ran, not stopping at all until he reached me. While changing clothes he jumped onto my shoes and using his beak and claws, climbed all the way onto the shoulder. If I was wearing a pair of shorts he climbed on the shoes and socks and then hung on whilst madly chirping away. Back on my shoulder he was quite happy to just sit there, quite often grooming and even taking a nap. This staying on me went further when at times he flatly refused to get onto the towel rack resulting with sleeping on my upper left arm. This was exactly the case when he had slept on me after I returned back from hospital. Being very aware of his presence, whenever I woke up or turned over, I was quite careful. I did my best not to disturb him. As soon as I resettled he did the same and as I started to dose off he chirped, I whistled and silence once again descended.

He never eased off from carrying out 'his duties' Often when he slept on the towel rack he woke me up at dawn by dropping down to the floor, which woke me up, ran into the bedroom and let go a couple of loud screeches. I lowered my hand to the floor, he jumped on and then he ran up to my forehead and proceeded to chirp to wake me. "I'm awake" I mumbled. Once he chirped and I responded, he went back to sleep either on my arm, forehead, or next to my ear if had I turned my head to the side. I wasn't far behind.

Due to medication, at times I needed a short afternoon nap. Without fail he joined me and slept on my arm. Imagine waking up half an hour later to see that he hadn't moved at all.

I was extremely pleased when 20 days later I noticed a major improvement in his attempts to fly. His descending flights off my shoulder to the floor, extended the distance of more than just a couple of feet. It definitely looked promising. I gleefully grabbed the phone and reported the news to the vet. She asked me to come over as soon as possible. Once again she checked him out, weighed him, and after a feather inspection was quite pleased with his progress. She gladly pointed out the new growth. She administered an injection, this time I was brave and my stress level didn't increase, mind you I didn't look either. Neither did I do so when she trimmed his claws. Weighing him showed that he had lost a fraction of his weight. This was put down to loss of muscle due to lack of flight. Medication was reduced now using only two types of drops of which one was a drop every second day. It was agreed to return back in 3 weeks and apart from another flight feathers inspection and discussion about eating proper food, he would most likely be taken off his medication.

During this period there were two incidents that completely surprised me, causing me to ask the question "How smart is a budgie?" It was also the incident that I couldn't stop laughing about, and I looked forward to telling anyone who was prepared to listen.

Every morning after I finished from the bathroom I went to the kitchen, prepared his medication and after cornering him, administered it. Of course this was under his continuous loud protest. Regularly as clockwork, as soon as I had finished the drops and released him, he quickly climbed and hid behind my neck. It was about a month since I had started his medication that this repetitive daily ritual taught him to run away as soon as I approached him. Keep in mind that it wasn't easy to catch him as I was still on crutches.

Living with Limpy

One Monday morning when I went looking for him I just simply failed to locate him. I looked everywhere, baffled, wondering where the heck he was. I checked his 'walkabout' in the bathroom, bedroom, lounge and kitchen. I walked up and down the hallway; I looked at every nook and cranny but to no avail. I walked back and forth in all of the rooms mentioned. I knew he hadn't flown away nor escape outside as I hadn't opened any outside doors at all. He had to be here. On my third run, which by now was very worrying I heard a faint whistle. It was so soft that it was barely audible. I looked in that direction and just broke up laughing. Believe it or not Limpy actually had stepped inside a boot, crouched, and hid from me. He had done a good job because there was no way of spotting him. His innocent 'G'day' hello gave him away.

The other incident caused me to ask the question "How can such birds with such a tiny mind, small enough that we insult a human by calling him a bird brain, could possibly know when a person is in pain without any visible outward sign?

Shortly after he was able to execute a downhill flight from my shoulder I had to spend one night in hospital following a minor nose operation. The following evening back home I once again settled down to watch TV, with Limpy as usual staying either on my shoulder or moving about on me. At one stage he moved to the middle of my right arm, resting on my chest and reaching on tip toes, attempted to groom the tip of my nose. Instinctively I pulled back being quite aware of a pain filled nose. A few moments later I relaxed and returned to watch TV. Once again I saw Limpy attempting to groom my nose. This time although being quite cautious, I let him do so. I was completely surprised, even perhaps lost for words as he started to groom the nose so gently, so softly, in such a caring way that it was like a butterfly kiss. I was supposed to be looking after him and instead he was consoling me. Later that night in bed I once again marvelled wondering how was it possible. Are birds so in touch with whatever is around them than they have the ability to know more than we give them credit for?

As the weeks passed I could see his flights were getting longer. Although still not gaining height he was able to cover more ground before landing on the carpet. The days of dropping down like a brick were over. And then one day it all came together. I was in the kitchen making a coffee and Limpy was on the counter. As usual he was walking around inspecting everything I was doing. I had to place my hand to block him getting any closer as I poured myself a coffee. Just as I was stirring my coffee he walked to the edge of the counter and took off. I expected him to fly a certain distance and then land on the carpet. It definitely wasn't the case this time, how wrong I was.

Yes, Limpy did take off and lose some height but then he flapped his wings and gained height so effortlessly, so elegantly that I stopped stirring my coffee and just froze in wonder as he gracefully landed on the lounge room curtain rod. "Wow" I joyfully cried out, "that was great, well done mate". I think that Limpy too was just as surprised by this action because he turned around and flew down back to the kitchen counter. He once again turned round and repeated his flight. I think that he was doing it again to convince himself.

It had been just on ten weeks since that unforgettable day, and now the sound of flapping wings could once again be heard. Limpy was airborne again doing high speed flybys; and he was enjoying it. His flight route was back to normal. From the bathroom, right through the bedroom, a sharp bank to the right, cross the hallway, another sharp bank to the right, past the lounge room, into the dining room and full speed straight ahead towards the kitchen. The flight was always the same, a quick stop on the kitchen window sill radio to survey the scene, followed by a quick drink and a bite to eat. Mission completed, and then it was a return flight back to his friend in the mirror or a quick hello to either one of my ears. Alternatively, leaving his bathroom mirror friend, he flew around looking to make sure I was still around, and either spends time with me or return back to his mirrored mate.

It was all smiles at the veterinary clinic the following day when Limpy was given a clean bill of health. Aside from Limpy's health we talked about writing an article about Limpy for publication.

On the way home even the traffic lights were turning green as I approached them. Well the sun was certainly shining that day. A package was waiting inside the letter box addressed to him. It contained a Christmas card and a couple of small bags of cuttle fish. We were both surprised; as a matter of fact Limpy was lost for words!

With the vets' instructions, the New Year period was difficult on me. It wasn't easy hiding human food from him. He accepted missing out on so many fast foods such as McDonalds and traditional British French fries which were a particular favourite, but really put up a fight when he saw me eating a slice of toast with vegemite. I wished I had filmed the scenario seeing a budgerigar madly screeching as loudly as possible trying to bypass my hand, completely focused on getting his beak on some vegemite. Eventually for peace and quiet I stopped having vegemite. Numerous suggestions both from the internet budgie group that I belonged to and the veterinarian, suggesting fruit and vegetables didn't help. Apart from human food Limpy flatly refused to eat anything other than one type of seed.

On the second visit to the clinic the vet had strongly suggested that Limpy should be given a vitamin A injection as a supplement. Two months after Limpy was back flying again I took him, this time in the transport cage back to the clinic.

Provided we're travelling in the car he didn't mind being in the cage but as soon as we arrived, he wanted out. A moment after I sat down in the waiting room he started putting up a fight, looking around trying to find a way out.

Whistling didn't help. By accident I found that the only way to calm him down was for me to insert a finger between the bars. As soon as I did he instantly jumped on it. In that position he completely calmed down. Another pet owner looked surprised saying that it looked as if I had thrown a switch. He came over and had a closer look at Limpy. He said that we must understand each other because he had never seen such animal behaviour.

Limpy was once again given a check-up and notes were typed into the computer. As expected I looked the other way as a hypodermic needle was plunged into his tiny body. Instead of placing him back in his cage the vet released him. Limpy flew over and once again hid behind my neck. The vet shook her head stating that Limpy was the only bird she knew of who knew where he was going to fly to.

There was no doubt about it; Limpy was certainly enjoying his new found freedom. He thoroughly enjoyed flying about. At times he flew doing figure eights around the rooms till his body said 'enough I need a rest'. He once again resumed flying over to me as soon as the phone rang. Picture me leaning on crutches asking questions and doing my best to hear the other party while Limpy was on my shoulder merrily joining in whistling and chirping. If the other party didn't know Limpy, then an inquiry was raised about hearing the sounds of a budgerigar.

Yes life had certainly returned back to normal.

Chapter 11

By Easter 2010 I could see changes taking place. After being on two crutches since April 2007 I took my first tentative step using just one crutch. If you think that was an achievement, the highlight was the ability to cross my leg when sitting down. Oh what joy, something that is taken for granted but hadn't been able to be executed for three years.

Limpy too was now benefitting from the vitamin A injection and he truly was a delight to observe. At times when he landed on the kitchen radio he seemed to adopt a 'pose' just for my benefit. He stood upright, proud and erect, perhaps even stretching his body making himself look taller. He absolutely looked magnificent. The smooth curvature of the head, neck and the swooping, flowing lines all the way down to the tip of the tail seemed more pronounced. A study in streamlining, a photograph begging to be taken! If ever there was a picture worth a thousand words this certainly was it. How could anyone not fall in love seeing such a picture of health?

I wondered that as he grew older he grew wiser or whether the vitamin A was the cause.

When Brenda, my carer came over, Limpy would land on the back of the sofa very close to where she was sitting. At times he would jump and land on her. He wouldn't stay there for long just enough for her to know that he was around. As friendly as he was to her in the lounge room, it was a different story in the bathroom. He would just stay on the shower screen frame, just eyeing her carrying out her chores. He wouldn't chirp or whistle or fly about, he would just watch and observe her. Without fail, as soon as she tried to clean the bathroom mirror, the mirror that he spent countless hours arguing with his mate in, Limpy would instantly loudly screech. Loud wasn't the word to describe his action. I could hear him from the other end of the house and on one occasion George from across the street said that he heard him screeching. Limpy made sure that Brenda knew of his disapproval.

As soon as she walked out of the room, the screeching stopped. Thankfully Limpy would fly onto her shoulder; she would bring him back to me. Without Limpy's supervision, Brenda would continue where she left off.

Apart from me, Brenda was the person often seen by Limpy. He kept her at arm's length. Over time, he did on a few occasions accept her and fly to her but he definitely put his foot down when it came to her being in the bathroom. I was the only one allowed to touch the mirror.

Another change that took place was whenever he was very active, and needed to cool down. Normally he would move his wings away from his body as a means of cooling down. One rather hot day upon arriving home I whistled as I placed my keys and loose change on the kitchen counter. There was no loud chirping or high speed flapping heading my way. So time for me to go and look for him. I looked around but I couldn't locate him. Oh no, not again, what is he up too, where's he's hiding now. Partially blocked by the shower door frame, Limpy was in the shower. One look at him and I had a chuckle.

When I shower I use a sponge rather than a wash cloth. Limpy was crouched down on the sponge with his wings away from his body enjoying a cool feeling on his stomach. A rather unique way of cooling down! Walking up to him I invited him to step on my finger. Ha, no such luck, he was enjoying it, and had no intention of moving at all.

So I just briefly caressed his wing and walked away.

Later in the afternoon when the air conditioner was pressed into service and the house started to cool down, I laid down for a nap. Hardly had my head touched the pillow when a loud chirp followed by flapping wings, saw Limpy land on my arm. "Aha" I said, "now that the room is cooler you want to be friends again". He casually walked onto my head and chirped a few times. I returned the compliment by a few whistles and closed my eyes. I heard him whistle again in the softest of ways. It was barely audible. A moment later I was asleep. Forty minutes later I woke up and he was asleep on my shoulder.

My cousin Tony and his wife Cherry popped in to see Limpy. What do you mean 'to see Limpy' I remarked, don't I count? Tony laughed saying that he was doing a follow up to see how Limpy was progressing after his 'damaged feathers' episode. As they sat down, Limpy was having a bite to eat. After making them a coffee, I sat down with them. Limpy's flight back onto my shoulder saw Tony comment about how healthy he looked. Cherry agreed stated that this was much better than being bitten. I turned around

Budges at times do not want to be disturbed. Even though they are a social bird they do like their privacy. When Limpy wanted solitude he would warn me to stay away by opening his beak. At first I didn't know what it meant, seeing him back away as I got closer, helped me understand. The funny thing was that as soon as I turned my back to him, he flew onto my shoulder.

On the subject of biting; although budgerigars in captivity look cute they do bite. Biting occurs either as an exploratory or a defensive act. In the exploratory mode the bird will use his beak as the name implies – to explore.

Budges at times do not want to be disturbed. Even though they are a social bird they do like their privacy. When Limpy wanted solitude he would warn me to stay away by opening his beak. At first I didn't know what it meant, seeing him back away as I got closer, helped me understand. The funny thing was that as soon as I turned my back to him, he flew onto my shoulder.

On the subject of biting; although budgerigars in captivity look cute they do bite. Biting occurs either as an exploratory or a defensive act. In the exploratory mode the bird will use his beak as the name implies – to explore.

In the defensive mode the budgie bites from fear or from being harassed. Usually he will send out a warning by opening his beak.

There are three ways to stop him from biting. The first and most obvious is to not place any part of your body within the beak's reach. No matter how bonded you are with the bird, allow him his own space.

Secondly if he starts to bite, gently blowing on him until he lets go is the best way to deal with it. It doesn't hurt him, but it interrupts the biting by being just annoying enough.

Thirdly is to actually let him bite. As soon as he bites there's the natural tendency to pull away - don't - let him bite, it is that simple. However, make sure that you present an area where it isn't easy to get a good hold. Instead of a finger present a knuckle, it isn't easy to get the beak around the knuckle and apply pressure. You'll find that he'll be unable to bite because he's unable to open his mouth wide enough to use leverage.

Once he understands that his actions are proving fruitless he'll give up.

asking Limpy what he had to say for himself. Surprise, surprise, Limpy flew over landing on the back of the couch and stayed there. As we talked he approached their heads. One could easily see Tony's desire to see Limpy jump onto his shoulder but alas, he didn't venture any closer. It was the usual – at arm's length. I pointed out that Limpy had never bitten me; however he had at times, by opening his beak, signalled for me to stay away.

That night Limpy stayed up way past his bedtime. On numerous occasions if I had visitors he wanted to stay up. You could see him, his eyes were practically hanging out, but he flatly refused to go to bed. When Tony and Cherry left, Limpy turned in and I retired to the study.

When I went to bed I made the mistake of switching on the bedroom main light rather than the dimly lit bedside light. In an instant Limpy flew out straight onto me and then went to visit his mate in the bathroom mirror. A moment later he was madly chirping. I doubt whether he could see all of his reflection? So here I was about to step into bed and Limpy wanted to socialise. It was one o'clock in the morning, this little mate should be snoring his head off. I got up and switched off the bedroom light for about 10 seconds and when I switched it on again he thankfully flew back to the towel rack. I quickly switched it off and carefully made my way back to the bed.

He was just like a child; he knew that lights out meant lights out, but giving him an inch meant he would take a mile.

A few days later just as I was finishing my dinner a couple of mates popped over. At one stage one of them looked at me and asked if I had heard Limpy chirping. I said no, but it wouldn't surprise me if he had. Hardly had I stopped talking when Limpy chirped again and next second he showed up flying from a dark bathroom, through a dark bedroom and straight onto my shoulder. A moment later he started to chirp joining in with our chatting.

Just before midnight my mates stood up and were ready to leave. I tried to place Limpy on one of his favourite landing spots but he simply refused to leave me. As a matter of fact I could feel him tighten his grip on my finger. He then climbed onto my shoulder and again I felt him tighten his grip. I told them that I was unable to leave the house because Limpy had indicated that he was not planning to get off me. They laughed as I stood waving behind the front door security screen.

Shortly after they left I gathered the coffee cups, washed and cleaned the kitchen. Before walking to the study I took him to the bathroom placing him on the towel rack. His eyes just wanted to close but still he refused to leave me. I took him to his sleeping spot but as soon as I turned my back to him, he jumped back on my shoulder. He just wouldn't settle down.

I went to the study with Limpy still on my shoulder. Looking at him I thought that he would most likely sleep on me. I didn't stay long in the study. For one thing Limpy felt restless, constantly moving, his tail both touching my ear or cheek and on one occasion moved directly under my nose.

Rather than argue I decided to join him and went to bed. Undressing wasn't easy as I slowly peeled a T Shirt over my head all the while feeling him hanging on. As soon as I lay down in bed he moved to my upper arm and quickly settled down.

Medication time meant that I woke up earlier than he usually did. "Sorry to disturb you mate", I whispered as I once again went back to sleep. After a stretch he flew from me back to his usual spot in the bathroom. An hour later he flew over to start the day by firstly waking me up.

As autumn gave way to winter, Limpy further expanded his domain by finding a far more comfortable perch - the bathroom toilet paper roll. Having a softer base compared to any other landing spot it soon became a favourite spot. As the toilet roll dwindled down to a few sheets there was a noticeable absence from Limpy but, as soon as a new roll was inserted he immediately showed up. Many a time I walked into the bathroom to see him crouching down on the roll either asleep or almost asleep.

Another change that was far more dramatic left me speechless with a lump forming in my throat.

One day while I was watching TV Limpy flew over landing on my shoulder and then walked all the way down my arm to my hand. "What are you up too?" I smilingly said. Much to my shocked surprise Limpy started to vomit seeds all over my thumb. Hardly had he finished when I stood up, cleaned my thumb and reached for the phone. The vet's line was engaged. "This is urgent" I cried out. Impatiently, I immediately called my cousin Tony. Yippee, faith smiled at me; Tony would be at my door within the hour. "An hour, can't you show up sooner" I cried? "Frank, I haven't mastered the art of flying", was his sarcastic reply.

I paced as best as I could, waiting for the hour to pass. Limpy who once again was on my shoulder looked at me, most likely wondering why I was pacing the floor? Finally the sound of a car in the driveway announced Tony's arrival and I unlocked the door and waited. As Tony walked in, Limpy did a high speed dash to the bathroom. Tony immediately asked what happened, and while reporting, showed him the stained tissue. I wasn't amused when he laughed, but seeing my look of concern, he soon explained Limpy's behaviour.

I was speechless when he explained the fact that Limpy wasn't sick at all, but had regurgitated his food with the intention of feeding me. As glad as I was to know he was okay and felt rather honoured, I wasn't exactly thrilled to see the seeds covered in bile running down my thumb. Relieved that everything was all right with the world I relaxed. Tony said that he had never seen such behaviour. "I'm impressed," he continued "Limpy hasn't just bonded with you, now he wants to look after you".

Much to my joy and disgust he continued to 'feed" me on a regular basis.

The discussion at the vet's office regarding submitting an article about Limpy for publication finally materialised in the winter edition of Australian Birdkeeper Magazine. I proudly opened the magazine to the appropriate page and showed it to Limpy. There you are mate, two pages and a couple of photos, how about that, I whispered in his ear. Looking over my shoulder he looked at the magazine but said nothing, no interest whatsoever. That's gratitude for you.

A few days later I took Limpy to get his vitamin A injection. The vet gave him a clean bill of health stating that he was in top form. His weight was text book perfect and his wing muscles in tip top condition. Leaning against the counter she said "OK I'm ready, tell me". Dumbfounded I replied "tell you what?" She asked "what adventures or mischief had he gotten into. Is he still annoying the next door neighbour's cat?" I laughed and nodded. She said that he was certainly unique, a budgie that preferred vegemite and loved to annoy cats.

Next she trimmed his claws. She said that we're a pair, both having a damaged left leg. She also stated that we were in love with each other, evidenced by the abnormal screeching when being held. I asked for an explanation. She pointed out that birds will soon stop screeching but those that have strongly bonded will continue, because they believe that their mate will come to the rescue. I mentioned the regurgitation incident. She laughed and said that it doesn't surprise her. He's your mate, he wants to feed you. She let Limpy fly away watching him urgently flap, circle and land on my shoulder and hide behind my neck. Smilingly she said that Limpy did exactly what she knew he would do, fly and hide behind my neck. He was the only one of her patients that did so.

Once I was safely inside the car I opened the cage door. Limpy flew out landing on my shoulder. Thankfully he didn't stand on the steering wheel directly in my field of vision. Instead he moved about between the shoulders and also flew onto the back parcel shelf. He walked the length of the shelf while all the time looking out the back window.

Hardly had we entered the house, Limpy made a beeline to the nearest mirror, and started reporting his latest adventure to his mate.

The joy of seeing Limpy effortlessly fly about didn't last.

Chapter 12

One Monday, about two weeks after getting his vitamin A injection Limpy didn't look his normal alert self. During the morning I noticed that he started to sit in a hunched up position, and wasn't eating or drinking and didn't chirp at all. As a matter of fact by lunch time he hadn't spent any time on my shoulder at all. He didn't even fly over to see what food was being prepared for lunch. An inspection of his food bowl showed that no seeds had been touched. Alarmingly I noticed him shivering and then started to throw up. This wasn't food regurgitation, this was vomiting. That's it, stop lunch and ring the vet. Within the hour I was on the way to the vet.

I was surprised to see another vet present when I was called in. This wasn't Limpy's vet and just before I was about to ask for her, he introduced himself and an assistant.

He checked Limpy out all the while explaining the procedures to his assistant. He told us that Limpy's weight was text book perfect and feeling around his body said that he was in excellent condition. When he queried his name I pointed out that it was due to his deformed leg. That was when the assistant asked whether this is the Limpy in the magazine article. I nodded. Replying to questions, I mentioned that he hadn't touched any food or drink at all plus the shivering and vomiting.

At the end of the examination he said that the best thing to do would be to admit him into hospital. My heart skipped a beat. He said that later on today he would personally do some specialised crop feeding and crop wash and micro wet prep. He said that tomorrow morning he would inspect the droppings, followed by radiographic contrast studies, a barium examination and would be feed some medication. I wasn't even listening much less understood what he was saying. I just kept on dumbly nodding. It's bad enough that I had been in hospital on a number of occasions, but now, my mate, he was so small. Continuing on I was informed that I should ring after 3 pm the following day for an update but the plan was to keep him till Wednesday late afternoon. He said that it was best to keep him under supervision for 48 hours. He said that Limpy would be intravenously fed with a number of inspections taking place throughout the day.

As if in a trance I just nodded.

The vet pointed out that when Limpy's vet reported for duty he would brief her on what was happening and pass Limpy onto her care. He assured me that Limpy would be taken care of with round the clock attention. He explained that he would be placed inside a large cage which had a plastic front and would be heated very much like a baby's humid crib. He stated that he was quite aware how much Limpy had bonded to me; I shouldn't worry, he was in very good hands. He smiled and said that it wasn't every day that the hospital had a celebrity.

An animal hospital admission isn't exactly cheap lodgings, but this was my mate, I was responsible for him, he took priority. Never mind, the car engine tune up it could wait for just a while longer.

For some reason as soon as I arrived back home I looked at the kitchen clock. Wednesday afternoon, that meant that I would either return then with Limpy, or empty handed. Sitting down I switched on the TV. It was noisy yet the house was so quiet. With no one to disturb, if tonight or Tuesday night I had to get up in the middle of the night I didn't have to use the visitor's toilet, I could just use the on-suite. "Some consolation" I spoke out.

When I rang on Tuesday I was informed that he was showing promise, he had started nibbling at food.

The message down the line on Wednesday afternoon was music to my ears. Limpy was AOK, my vet said, come and pick him up. "Your bird just doesn't want to sit still. He's merrily chirping keeping the other sick birds awake and he's hopping up and down trying to find a way out of the cage."

"Yep, that sounded like Limpy", I loudly proclaimed. "I'm on my way" I replied, placing the phone down before I had finished talking. "How much do you want to bet that every traffic light will be red?" I spoke out loud as I reversed the car out of the garage. I was right, blasted lights.

At the vet's I handed my cage to an assistant. She came back with Limpy facing her. As soon as she turned the cage around and saw Limpy, I whistled, he chirped and ran to the corner nearest me. Immediately he started to climb the bars trying to fight his way out. I poked one finger between the bars and instantly he jumped on my finger and just stood perfectly still. Two girls with a dog in the waiting room gasped, seeing Limpy's reaction and commented upon it. When I started to pull my finger out so I could move the cage and prepare to pay I could feel Limpy's claws tightening their grip.

I was given some medication to use twice a day for 5 days. The vet came out and said that she was perfectly happy with him, very healthy, and he put on 0.03gram in weight. I laughed; "someone must have sneaked in with a pizza" I replied. She laughed too, telling me to call her in a week's time for her own benefit, call sooner if there's a problem.

By the time I put the cage on the back seat the sun had gone down. From the front seat I leaned back and started to open the cage door. Limpy had no patience whatsoever; as soon as it was partially opened he literally ducked under the door and ran up my arm. Oh ok, I guess you're ready to go. Limpy stayed on my left shoulder for some time before he moved to the right and started looking out of the side window. It wasn't long before he ran down my arm to the wrist. He decided that the time had come for me to scratch the back of his head. So here was I driving along a three lane divided road, holding the steering in the left hand with a bird sitting on my wrist and performing grooming duties using my right finger. I didn't believe this. I was actually glad when he pulled away assuming he was satisfied when a moment later he walked along the steering wheel to my right hand and presented his head to do the other side. I was glad there was no police presence. If they saw this happening I'm sure I would have been pulled over. Try explaining my action to two unsmiling officers of the law.

With the engine switched off, the garage door closed and all the lights switched off, I walked into the house with Limpy still on my shoulder. I assumed that he would fly to see his mates in the mirror but he steadfastly stayed on my shoulder. I walked into the bedroom to change. As soon as I took off one piece of clothing he jumped back onto me. Changing clothes wasn't easy with him hanging on; he flatly refused to get off me. Back in the kitchen I topped up his food and water containers. It was quite heartening to see him getting stuck into his food once again.

Living with Limpy

As soon as he had his fill he flew back onto my shoulder and didn't move from there. Looking at him, his eyes were half closed, he was practically asleep. I took him to the bathroom a couple of times. He got on my finger and then onto the towel rack but as soon as I turned around he flew back onto my shoulder. OK mate, you can sleep with me tonight.

He once again slept on my left upper arm.

Limpy wasn't on me when I woke up. Looking around I saw him crouched in a ball on the toilet paper roll. Oh no, warning bells started ringing again. I had a quick shower, all the time wondering what was going on with him. Back in the kitchen I was happy to see him eat but was quite concerned observing him with an unusual leg movement, very similar to a person trying to kick start a motorcycle. Strange, I've never seen that happen. In the course of 30 minutes he seemed obsessed about it, moving his leg up and down against his body. I rang the vet and was told to bring him in. All this time he didn't chirp at all.

The vet said that the last thing she expected to see was Limpy since yesterday he was quite chirpy. My explanations of his actions at home and seeing first hand herself resulted in admitting him back in hospital. The vet said that a blood sample would be taken and analysed. I was told to ring later in the day for the result.

She pointed out that this behaviour wasn't normal and she said that she suspected that Limpy might be suffering from testis problems ranging from an inflamed testis to possible cancer. X-rays were also to be taken. She further stated that surgery wasn't advisable.

I've lost my appetite that day. When I rang I was informed that the results hadn't come through. Every few minutes I looked at the phone.

Just before lunch time the next day I rang the vet and was very disappointed to hear that the report hadn't come through. I decided to go and see her. If anything at least I could see Limpy. When I arrived 40 minutes later I was told that the report had come through. A few minutes later I was summoned into her office. First were the X-Rays, great news everything inside the body was where it should be and NO major problems at all. All the organs were healthy. Ask me whether I was relieved. Next was the blood test report. She explained quite a number of variations which didn't make sense. The good news there was that Limpy was very healthy; his cholesterol level was text book perfect. White blood cells were slightly up due to trauma. This went on for a few more minutes before she said something that 'clicked'.

I pointed out that on both Saturday and Sunday I woke up just in time to see Limpy fly from the bathroom towel rack to the bedroom curtain rod. As it was still practically dark flying from a partially lit room into a dark room he misjudged the distance, didn't succeed in reaching the curtain rod and had fallen down to the ground. I put this down to 'night flying' and dismissed the incident. As she was about to speak she was interrupted and had to take a phone call. She asked the nurse to take me to see Limpy till she came back.

I'm sure my smile was from cheek to cheek as I spotted Limpy in the humid crib. The nurse called out "Limpy, you have a visitor" As she slid opens the cage plastic door I whistled to him and lowered my finger towards him. Limpy jumped onto my finger and ran and I mean RAN as fast as he could up to my shoulder and hid at the back of my neck. The nurse commented on his high speed run. She left and I was left alone with Limpy. He didn't chirp, didn't move at all and when I tried to get him onto my finger he just pulled away and stayed just at the back and out of reach. We stayed like that for around 10 minutes in complete silence.

When the vet returned to put him back in the cage he avoided her hands and steadfastly refused to move anywhere. When she finally got him his screeching was the loudest I'd ever heard. He was protesting and in the highest pitches possible. He put up a fight. An inspection of the wing feathers had revealed that Limpy had once again, thankfully, slightly damaged his flight feathers. This has resulted in being unable to gain better lift, which explained why he had failed to make it to the curtain rod. Apart from that his madly flapping has resulted in over stressing his flight muscles which caused an increase in white blood cells. That explained why on Monday he was huddled up, not eating or chirping because he was in pain.

Suddenly everything in the report was falling into place. When I took him back the second time and the vet saw his "kick starting" leg movement she was mystified and later found out the cause. Because he was fed intravenously the solution was slightly runnier to help it go through his system. What had happened was his droppings didn't completely drop partially because of his abundant rear grouping of feathers. This had resulted in a buildup of dropping and partially blocked the anal passage. This was the explanation for why he was trying to "kick" the problem away. Once he was cleaned up and the offending feathers removed he was given a slight 'shaving' of the area.

Good heavens - a bird that needs shaving. Blasted Limpy, he had to be different or difficult! The vet laughed saying yep that's Limpy for you, just doing his best to worry you.

The vet said that she would keep him overnight and after morning inspection, subject to her complete satisfaction, would release him by lunchtime.

I walked on air, as I was leaving the hospital. Suddenly I felt hungry. Back home I noticed the flashing light on the answering machine and found two messages inquiring about Limpy's condition. Hardly had I finished lunch when I heard knocking on the front door from my neighbour wanting to know the latest about Limpy.

When I went to pick him up I was told that within the hour he had started to normally eat and drink. The vet was quite happy with his progress; he had started to put on weight too. He had been given an injection plus would be given mouth drops. I still had to administer the medication and she would want to see him again in three days' time for a final checkup.

It was late afternoon when I brought Limpy back home.

On Sunday the house once again reverberated to his loud chirping and noisy arguments with his mates in the mirrors. Yippy the nightmare was over. I certainly didn't want to go through all that again.

I once again enjoyed seeing him fly about or staying on my shoulder merrily chirping, great to see him back to full health. There was no doubt about it I loved this bird and knew that he loved me too. We're world apart yet have one thing in common, a damaged left leg.

One thought upset me. When he was in hospital the house was so quiet, and worse, I felt so lonely. It was going to be a sad day when he passed away. Yes I could easily replace him but there was no way I would have another one like him. He was truly a unique bird.

The following day I woke up to hear Limpy having one very loud argument with his bathroom mirror mate. I didn't know what the argument was about but Limpy was definitely giving his mate a piece of his mind. He was so vocal about it. Yep, he was definitely back to his usual self. I got out of bed and went over to see what the commotion was all about. Limpy was moving his head back and forth and flying and landing back onto the mirror's frame. I just leaned against the wall and watched. I also saw some tearing of the toilet paper. He had been on the toilet roll. This was something new, using the paper roll as a landing zone. As I was about to leave the room Limpy flew over and started to groom my left ear. Oh that's nice, one moment you're arguing with your mate and then gave him a quick brush off.

I changed my breakfast from vegemite toast to cereal. Apart from a change, I wanted to take away Limpy's vegemite temptation. Some of these cereals taste like cardboard so apart from adding milk I also added sultanas, peanuts and cashews for taste. As expected, Limpy showed up but seeing no vegemite present flew off. To him this was totally unsatisfactory and within a week I was in for a surprise. He tasted the milk.

Limpy approached the bowl and actually raised himself on 'tip toes'. Just a drop mind you and clearly could see that he wasn't sure whether he liked it, his beak was rapidly moving about. He then actually dipped his beak back in the milk tasting it once again. What was this, milk sampling? I don't think he could make up his mind. A moment later, the unbelievable was happening right in front of my eyes. He left the milk alone and attempted to pick up a cashew? This wasn't happening; of all the sultanas, peanuts and cashews around he had to select the largest one around. Typical, Limpy's eyes were bigger than his stomach. Blasted bird, he was trying to steal it. Of course it was too large to carry in his beak. He tried and tried again; eventually giving up. A few moments later he tried again and unsuccessful in his attempt, flew away, loudly protesting. He returned a few minutes later landing on my shoulder then off again landing on his seed container. "What a letdown" I cried, from cashews to seeds.

Hardly had he finished when he saw the next door neighbour's Siamese cat looking through the kitchen window. Limpy once again flew over landing on the kitchen radio and again proceeded to parade up and down among the knobs, switches and dials teasing the cat without mercy. The cat, by now should have learned just sat and watched, dreaming of a quick meal, so near yet so far away. As expected the cat dejectedly walked away when Limpy was out of sight having flown back to the bathroom after toying with the poor animal. You'd reckon the cat would have learned by now.

Living with Limpy

Aside from the cat the problem of breakfast was still there. I then remembered that when I was holidaying in America in the late nineties I was introduced to a fruit cocktail for breakfast. Why not I thought, yes I would buy a variety of fruit and introduce them to Limpy. Yes healthy living for him from now on.

So the following morning I placed an apple neatly sliced, 4 beautiful blood red strawberries and a sliced banana on a plate. I also placed a still unopened tub of strawberry yogurt. Before I had a chance to whistle Limpy over, he showed up. Off course, with so much food present I bet he smelt it and there was no way he was going to miss this opportunity.

I would have loved to see him help himself to the fruit - nah, no such luck; he flew down by passing everything, didn't even have a second glance and walked over to the tub of yogurt. It was still sealed and he walked around it looking for an opening. "Look mate, look at all this food, its yummy" I stated. No need to bother talking; he was suffering from selective deafness. He just kept on circling the tub poking it here and there trying to find an opening. Hardly had I peeled the lid when he unceremoniously inserted his beak. A bird with strawberry yogurt stain on his beak, what else does one do but laugh? He ate some, walked away, turned around and walked back for a tiny bit more. He walked around aimlessly looking like he was undecided whether to have any more. What was funny, what really cracked me up was his rapidly moving beak. It really looked like he was 'smacking his beak'. This walking around went on one more time before he took off and flew onto the kitchen radio. I was too busy laughing to eat.

Over the years I had hoped that Limpy would eat a wider variety of seeds but alas that wasn't the case. His love for human food still surprised me. Part of me just like any parent watching a child was happy seeing him eat yet I also knew that human food wasn't good for him.

> Although budgies can't process dairy products yogurt has some vitamins that are good for budgies but are to be given very sparingly

One way to stop temptation was to have my dinner later than normal, an hour or so after he 'turned in' for the night. This move proved successful but not perfect. There was always the odd occasion when Limpy made an appearance.

Living with Limpy

One evening, way after Limpy went to 'bed' I settled down in front of the TV with my favourite, Chinese take away. As soon as I sat down the phone rang and a mate, Peter, told me that he was on his way over after he picks up some McDonalds. I laughed saying that I too had just picked up some takeaway.

Hardly had I sat down again and picked up the fork when out of a darkened bedroom Limpy flew out at full speed landing on my right shoulder. "What is this mate, you are able to smell Chinese food from three rooms away?" I whispered. He wasn't in a talking mood. I had seen this before; as soon as he saw food he got selective deafness. A moment later he ran down my arm stopping just short of the fork. Balancing on the food container he walked around it nibbling on anything that had cooled down.

Shortly after, Peter walked in with his McDonald takeaway. As soon as he sat down and started to unwrap his food Limpy flew over onto his shoulder. I had to laugh. Peter turned around and said "Aha so you only want to know me when I have food in my hands". Limpy once again, true to his form didn't listen, as a matter of fact he didn't even look at Peter; he just walked down his arm and started nibbling the French fries.

Two grown men just sitting down watching a bird eat first Chinese cuisine followed by McDonalds. What a combination. I don't know who was worse, the humans or the bird?

After Limpy had his fill he surprised us by flying back onto Peter's shoulder. There was no chirping, no grooming, just a satisfied bird following such an assorted fine meal. A few minutes later he flew onto the TV set. That was my signal to get up, walk past Limpy heading towards the bedroom and give out a short sharp whistle. Sure enough, as played out numerous times before, as I whistled, Limpy flew onto my shoulder and I took him to the bathroom when he flew down onto the towel rack. By the time I walked back into the lounge room, I'm sure he was asleep.

Although I had changed my meal time, breakfast was another issue. After a rather considerably long delay I decided to revert to having toast for breakfast. Ah yes the smell of coffee and toasted vegemite bread was a welcoming scent. I didn't believe it, is it possible? Call it magic, witchcraft or voodoo but a moment later with one bite of the sliced bread being chewed; Limpy instantly appeared doing a high speed fly-by to my right shoulder. How is it conceivable that from 3 rooms and a period of 60 days later he could smell his favourite food? Is my budgie part blood hound?

No hello nor pardon me, he just ran down from my shoulder to the fingers and buried his head in the vegemite covered bread. Again as in previous times Limpy displayed absolutely disgusting behaviour, no table manners whatsoever. He attacked that bread as if it was going to be his last meal.

Well if you can't beat them join them. On rare occasions as a treat I would let him take a few tiny mouthfuls before I put a stop to it. To say he objected when it happened would be an understatement, he positively screeched loud and long before he returned back to the bathroom. You could hear him chirp and screech loudly as he reported his activities to his bathroom mirror mate. It was truly unbelievable behaviour for one so small.

I'm positive that where birds eat to live, Limpy lived to eat.

Chapter 13

September ah yes, the month where so many changes happened. Spring was here. Although the temperature was still low, to remind us of what winter was like, the promise of extra light, warmth and a more comfortable surrounds was noticeable. To me the start of this month was of major importance. Forty-one months and four operations had passed since my industrial accident and I took my first steps without using crutches. I didn't go far; as a matter of fact I found that I needed a walking stick but what an achievement. The physiotherapist's ear to ear grin said it all.

Limpy too was enjoying life, looking like he had a spring in his step. Well what do you expect? Spring is the time when all creatures' thoughts turn to sex. And a male budgie is no exception. Flying onto my right shoulder and like a dog wagging his tail, followed by a body stiffening action clearly showed me that I was more than a mate, I was his mate.

Grooming took on a new meaning as he started to moult. He turned himself into an acrobat as he twisted and turned this way and that fervently sprucing himself. Yep, it was time to change the wardrobe.

In a few short weeks all this was to change. I simply couldn't believe it. I didn't know whether to be angry, livid, and ropeable or just place my head in my arms and cry. Twenty one days after spring came in I found myself lying on a hospital gurney following a road accident. Ironically I felt fine and would have loved to go home but the left leg, the leg that for the last 41 months had seen four operations was once again broken in a couple of places requiring to be reopened and more steel plates and screws inserted. What had I done to deserve this?

The following morning, my brother Les and my mate Peter volunteered to alternately replenish Limpy's feed and water. I was grateful for their help pointing out that I would only be in hospital for a couple of days. Of course what was planned and what actually happened were two different things.

Moulting is seasonal. A caged budgie can moult once even twice a year, some budgies molt a little all year round, a couple of feathers at a time. But usually it happens at the start of spring/summer or autumn/ winter. The first moult will take place around 12 weeks. His first feathers are replaced by new ones; he also loses the appearance of a young bird. When he gets his new feathers the large, dark stripes across his head disappear.

During moulting the budgie does experience some stress. This is quite normal however, if the moulting is abnormally heavy and seems as if he's grooming far more than normal (like becoming obsessed about it) this might means that he's having a problem.

Spraying him with lukewarm water every day helps him to get the loose feathers out more easily.

If he's really becoming obsessed it helps to carry out an inspection of the flight feathers. Place the bird in your hand, place the index and middle finger on either side of the head and tip the budgie on his back. Gently spread the wing, he's going to object but it is not hurting him. Take a close look at his flight feathers, in particular look for any signs of damaged feathers such as fraying. If the bird is picking on his feathers most likely the new feathers are having trouble coming out to replace the old ones. Although you can help by removing the damaged feather it is best to take him to a vet. Remember the bird is most likely in pain. The vet should pull out any damaged feathers thus giving the new feather room to grow. The vet will probably give you drops to administer to help ease the pain.

On the second day following an operation I was informed that there would be another major operation taking place in two days' time. With a total of twenty five pieces of steel in the left leg my hospital stay would easily pass the fourteen day period.

I didn't believe this, this was a nightmare, all I want to do was go home and spend time with my mate and instead I was sentenced to spend more time away.

Every morning as the doctors carried through with their rounds I put up a logical argument reasoning that I should go home pointing out that irrespective of where I was I was still in the same amount of pain. My argument fell on deaf ears. Finally on the nineteenth day of begging, either they relented or I wore them out, and I was soon on my way home. You could not imagine how glad I was to return back home, more so to once again see Limpy. By now I was well aware that he was more than a pet. He gave me the incentive to return home as soon as possible. If there was no Limpy I would have gone to rehabilitation.

I suddenly felt anger as I entered the lounge room seeing the lounge chair and foot stool where I had spent so many months sitting in, nursing a broken left leg. I had to start physiotherapy and numerous pain killing tablets all over again. Yet a moment later my heart melted as I saw Limpy's droppings. Unlike previous hospital visits this time Limpy had stayed and slept on the back of my chair.

Oh my God, for the last nineteen days Limpy had patiently waited for me on my chair.

I looked for Limpy and found him waiting on my pillow. One look at him and I started crying. Limpy looked awful, once again his feathers looked matted, lacked colour and looked as if he had picked at his body feathers. He has stressed over my absence. I just couldn't stop crying. My brother was surprised to see me in this condition and consulted me thinking that I was crying as a result of the accident.

In between sobs I managed a rather weak whistle. That was all that was needed. Limpy took off straight onto my shoulder. His loud screeching preceded a rather enthusiastic grooming of my ear. My brother helped me back into the lounge room and switched on the TV. Shortly after my brother made me a coffee and left, I dozed off. When I woke up Limpy was still on my shoulder.

After having some seeds, he for some reason flew down to the ground in front of me and walked over. As soon as I whistled our familiar whistle he flew onto my foot and practically ran up my body all the way to my shoulder. Makes me wonder why he didn't just fly over. A moment later he started to chirp in my ear and again tears welled in my eyes. He kept on chirping stopping only to breakout into a song.

For the next few days he hardly got off me. Every morning he woke me up, I took my medication and went back to sleep. When I finally woke up again he was still on me. I had slowly washed myself with him on me; staying on me till I offered him a drink following shaving. He drank, then washed himself and flew off to the kitchen to say g'day to his mates. I slowly dress, it wasn't easy wearing an arm and leg brace, and it seemed to take forever.

Once I had finished dressing I slowly make my way to the kitchen. He stayed on the kitchen radio, his eyes never leaving me, while I prepared his seeds and as soon as he had eaten, flew back on to my shoulder.

Three days later and he was still spending practically every waking moment on me, even when I went to lie down in the afternoon to rest the leg; he just sat on my upper arm and stayed there till I got up again. It was like having a watch dog. How did he know I was in pain?

Within a week I came to terms that I had to start physio all over again. By that same time Limpy was looking much better. His coat once again glistened especially when the sun was on him; he stood proud and erect and looked a picture of health.

One of my first visitors was Marian, my next door neighbour. Once again she did my shopping and came over for a coffee keeping me company. An animal lover she owned a dog and the beautiful Siamese cat, she enjoyed watching Limpy and thoroughly loved his behaviour. She gladly volunteered to look after him changing his food and water on the rare occasion I had to be away overnight. The bopping of his head and loud chirping when he wanted to join in our conversation was more than cute; she looked forward to seeing it again and thoroughly loved it. He flew onto the back of her chair but never jumped on her shoulder. She believed that he could smell the cat on her.

When I said that it would be quite some time till I could return to a full time job she stated that Limpy would certainly miss me since in her eyes Limpy and I were very lucky to have each other. She said that it isn't often to see an owner and a bird share the same disability, more so to see such a strong bond between them.

The following week I was, once again leaving home, immediately after a quick breakfast (or none at all) reporting to the physiotherapist and spending a few hours away from Limpy. I always looked forward to returning back home as I felt it was the only safe place. As soon as I entered the house I whistled and sure enough Limpy would come out flying at full speed back onto my shoulder. What a welcoming gesture. This was something I would never tire off.

One afternoon when I whistled he didn't come over so I went looking for him. As soon as I entered the bedroom and saw him on the bathroom toilet roll he flew off onto the bathroom radio. This had happened before but this time I felt that I had caught him doing something. It was quite clear that I had startled him.

As soon as I sat down on the bed to change he flew over onto my shoulder. I broke up laughing, looking at him as if I could read his mind. Clearly he was up to something and knowing Limpy as I did, he definitely was not behaving.

Unlike a dog which has the ability to show an emotion such as the lifting of the eyebrows, a budgie has a poker face; it is void of any expressions. I can only guess what happened by seeing some sort of result.

The hours passed but the nagging feeling that I caught him out persisted. It wasn't till I silently walked back into the bathroom that I discovered what he had been up too. There right in front me I saw the results. Limpy had torn a small hole in the toilet paper. He has been nibbling it. I thought nothing of it till a few days later when I found more evidence of Limpy nibbling the toilet paper roll.

The next time Limpy was on my shoulder I said that this new toilet paper craze should stop, pointing out that surely you could do something that wasn't destructive. Did he listen – no, not at all? The day after when I noticed that he wasn't flying around and instead rather quiet, I went to investigate and sure enough he was back on the toilet paper roll.

The long Cup Day weekend gave me the time to take Limpy once again for a check-up and the required vitamin A injection. Once again I was pleased to hear that he passed with a clean bill of health but surprised to find out that Limpy had put on weight. Limpy had gained 3 grams. One couldn't blame him, he lived to eat, and it was inevitable. "OK young fella you're going on a diet when we arrive back home".

Living with Limpy

The return trip was predictable; I kept an eye out on traffic and another on a bird that spent time flying from my shoulders to the back parcel shelf where he paraded to the delight of passers-by.

An Australian budgie, in peak condition and able to fly unhindered, his weight is between 42 to 44grams. Limpy was at 47 grams.

In regards to weight loss this is quite simple. First place him in a cage by himself. Buy measuring spoons and fill one with seeds and place the seeds in the appropriate container. The following day see whether he has eaten them all or not. If he has, use the same amount the following day. If he hasn't, use the same spoon again but this time instead of bulging with seeds, level the amount. Once he's able to finish a level spoon than slowly reduce the amount again. Then go down to a smaller measuring spoon and so on. There's no hurry to do this, it's not a race, take your time. The budgie will slowly but surely lose weight. Once he starts to lose weight he will rapidly shed it.

Remember that as he's shedding weight he will also be losing vitamins/minerals so install a piece of cuttle fish as a supplement.

A month later I took him to be weighed and was pleased with the results. Limpy had successfully dropped his weight back to where it was supposed to be. He was looking a picture of health - trim, taut and terrific. "Great mate" I said, "just in time to start putting it back on thanks to the Christmas festivities". The vet laughed as once again Limpy flew back to my shoulder.

Christmas was soon upon us and it was quite a busy time. Not for Limpy, he couldn't have cared less. He was still busy chatting or arguing to his mirror mates, crowded me while I showered, shaved and dressed and never showed any mercy to the next door neighbour's cat by still parading in front of him. Poor Dobbie, so close yet so far away.

When a coin is dropped onto a hard surface such as concrete or tiles it produces a distinctive sound. This was the sound that I heard one day while I was in my study. Such an unusual sound caused me to place my hands on my pants pockets before I realised that I didn't have any money on me. When I arrive home I always empty my pockets, placing the wallet and loose change on the kitchen counter. There was no sound of flapping wings or loud chirping so this sound needed to be investigated, but I could clearly guess who was causing it.

Sure enough, as soon as I cautiously peaked around the corner into the kitchen I caught Limpy red handed. With his beak he was busily pushing the 5 and 10 cent coins to the edge of the counter and watching them fall down to the floor. What does one do in this situation other than shake one's head in disbelief? I entered the room and slowly sat down never once taking my eyes off him. A coin is observed hitting the floor; Limpy turned around, walked over to the next coin and started the procedure again. The trip to the edge wasn't always in a straight line but Limpy kept on persisting, pushing the coin to the edge and beyond. When the final coin had stopped spinning he looked up, turned around, and flew off. Another chore finished – what's next on the agenda?

What did I do? What else could I do except laugh as I cautiously supporting myself on my crutches bent down to pick up the coins. It didn't last, no more than fifteen minutes later I once again heard the unmistakeable sound of coins falling. I broke out laughing. Leave them on the floor, they can't fall any further.

A week later I saw the postman drop in a parcel. Opening it I found a present addressed to Limpy. He had received a present all the way from Arizona, USA. Now that was a most pleasant surprise. Roxanne Harshman, a member of the Internet Budgie Group sent Limpy a bird's swing. Limpy has a fan from the other side of the world. I walked back inside and with the swing raised above my head called him over. No response. Oh – oh this is most unusual. Limpy always flew over. I know he heard me. Not flying over meant one thing, he was up to something.

On crutches I walked towards the bathroom, looking in the most obvious places where he hung out. I found him just sitting on the bathroom radio. I also found one damaged roll of toilet paper. In the past he had nibbled on the roll with the resulting four or five sheets of paper being thrown out. Not this time. Limpy had shown no mercy whatsoever and started to tear the roll making a single hole and widening it as he burrowed through. As soon as he saw me he flew over onto my shoulder and merrily started chirping as if to say that nothing was out of the ordinary and there was no carnage. I just looked at him and shook my head in disapproval then started to unroll the toilet paper and throw away the damaged sheets. They were not at all useful if the middle of each sheet was torn away. Thirty-seven sheets gave up their lives that afternoon.

The start of the toilet paper saga

It must have been the Christmas Spirit because Limpy surprised me again.

As previously mentioned he had surprised me years ago when he mimicked my whistle. That tune was used quite often by me especially when I returned back home. As time passed he imitated other tunes except one. The other ones he went as far as mixing them up, lengthening, and even modified them. Every time I heard him I stopped what I was doing and enjoyed listening and marvelled as he played the lengthened version. Even visitors stopped talking when they heard his repertoire.

Still, unfortunately one tune was missing. No matter how much I whistled it he just didn't mimic it. Then finally out of the blue, four years later on my birthday he let go with a superb rendition. He was sitting on the back of my chair. It was played out clearly and loud enough that there was no way I could have ever missed it.

What a lovely birthday present. Finally after close to three years on the last day of the year he finally whistled it. I didn't know whether to say 'well done' or 'about time'.

Regrettably Limpy whistled it once and only once. No matter how many times I whistled it he simply never whistled it again. Now I wonder whether he whistled it to show me that he could do it or just to shut me up.

The tune was the internationally recognised 'Wolf Whistle'.

Chapter 14

The first day of the year means a lot to people. In my case since my birthday is on the last day of the year the first day of the New Year means it's a long way to my next birthday. In Limpy's case his birthday was nine months away. To Limpy, himself, it was just another day. Another day of seeing what mischief he could get himself into.

It didn't take long. Just on lunch time I became aware that the house was very quiet, that meant he's up to something. A room to room check ended in the bathroom with pieces of toilet paper scattered around the tiled floor. The roll, or I should say what remained of the roll of paper didn't look the best either. "Oh mate", I cried. Instantly he flew over landing on my shoulder and started to groom my ear. Ah yes, trying to sooth the savage beast eh! "What am I going to do with you?" I said, "I can't close the door otherwise you'll either not be able to enter your room or get out of it". Looking at the sorry sight I decided to leave it and clean up later.

As soon as I entered the kitchen Limpy flew onto the radio and didn't once take his eyes off me. Naturally, I was preparing food, his favourite hobby.

Apart from a family visit, that first day was memorable for an incident that happened involving Limpy – who else?

For whatever reason Limpy refused to go to bed at dusk, he stayed on my shoulder a few hours way past his bedtime. One look at him and you could see his eyes wanted to close; yet he battled to keep his eyes open. I took him to his room, placed him on the towel rack but as soon as I turn around he would fly back on me. Eventually I accepted the situation knowing that this wasn't the first time of going to bed where he would sleep on my left upper arm. Off course I could always just place him on his sleeping perch and switch off all the lights to prevent him from flying but it was a rather risky act walking back to the bed on crutches in pitch darkness.

So on the first night of the New Year he slept on my arm. When I woke up for my medication he woke up too but soon settled back on my arm when I lay down again.

Imagine my surprise when I next woke up to see Limpy directly in front of me. I couldn't believe it, I didn't want to move, and I even held my breath. I gently, very gently pulled my head back. There, directly in front of my eyes, was Limpy asleep, crouched down, his legs neatly tucked underneath on the pillow a few inches away from my face. I couldn't believe it, more so the actual placing. He was in a position where he wasn't being disturbed by exhaled air from both my mouth and nose.

I know I snore so how could he possibly sleep with such a racket going on a mere few inches away?

What a beautiful sight, there was no way I was going to say a word; I had a lump in my throat and briefly fought to hold back a tear. How positively beautiful and innocent he looked there peacefully sleeping, not moving a muscle. It certainly was a picture worth having. I looked at him, a smile forming across my face and telling myself how fortunate I was to have such a mate. I just kept on looking at him. Not wishing to disturb him I closed my eyes and went back to sleep.

When I woke up Limpy was on the curtain rod looking down at me and busily grooming his wings.

That summer Limpy carried on with his usual daily actions. As if he hadn't got enough activities in between high speed flights he found and definitely enjoyed carrying out a new pastime.

Shortly after I got Limpy I placed a small shaving mirror on top of the refrigerator. The idea was for Limpy to meet and have someone to talk too. When I introduced him to this mirror Limpy would approach it and started to chirp and gently touch the mirror with his beak. At times the chirping was loud, other times at a more accepted level. But at times this action would change. Limpy would slowly, almost cautiously walk up to the mirror, briefly touch it with his beak and then run away to the fridge door. It was as if he was trying to annoy the reflection and then run away before he was caught out. He would do this a number of times. At times he even walked towards the mirror but would go to the edge and 'peak' around as if to see the bird from the back. A moment later he would rush to the edge of the fridge and eventually take off. Now from this action it developed further.

Annoying the 'other bird'

On a warm summer's morning as I opened the fridge door Limpy left his mirror mate and jumped onto the fridge door. As it swung open he looked down at the floor. No big deal, I retrieved a cold item. But as soon as I started to close it he spun around and watched the floor again till the door was fully shut.

As I walked away from the fridge he walked back to the mirror but as soon as I approached the fridge he ran back onto the door. I thought it was strange perhaps funny but he started to repeat this movement. So keeping my eyes on him I walked away then returned. Sure enough as soon as I walked to the fridge he run away from the mirror and jumped onto the door and as I opened the fridge door he chirped and looked down as he swung with the opening door.

Again, as soon as I closed the door he spun around and again looked down towards the floor. Limpy was enjoying the movement of the door opening and closing. This was all well and good, but it wasn't helping the refrigerator keep a constant temperature. I had to put an end to it.

As soon as I walked away, he went back to the mirror; however as soon as I sat down for breakfast he flew straight onto my shoulder. Aha, meals on wheels. Food, that takes precedence over his mate in the mirror. Limpy knew his priorities.

The long hazy lazy days of summer kept Limpy awake for a much longer period. I must confess there were times when I was glad he turned in for the night. As much as I enjoyed his company on my shoulder, my ear deserved a break from the few hours of chirping and whistling.

It had long become a habit for my mate Peter to come over and visit me on Thursday nights. Although the TV stayed on we mostly looked at it if there was something of interest. The lounge room and kitchen lights remain switched on. One evening I made arrangements with him to pop over after dark to watch a very interesting TV programme. I told him that it was going to be shown late at night which means we can sit back without Limpy interrupting. My mate laughed and agreed and decided to pick up a pizza and a couple of beers to enjoy while watching the documentary. At the appropriate time all the house lights were switched off and with pizza in hand sat back to watch the programme.

No more than 10 minutes later Peter suddenly broke up laughing. I couldn't see why, as the scene on the screen was quite a dramatic one. Just as I turned to look at him a movement caught my eye. Limpy was walking into the room. I didn't believe this. Unable to fly due to the house being in darkness, he actually as casually as could be, walked from the bathroom, into the bedroom and proceeded towards the lounge room after crossing the hallway. Peter continued laughing when Limpy walked by, looked up at him and carried on towards me. I just momentarily sat there lost for words. I switched on the reading lamps and that was enough for Limpy to switch to flight mode and a moment later landed on my hand. Oh no, not his usual landing zone, the shoulder, but my hand. But of course that's where the pizza slice was. For goodness sake, no way mate; no pizza for you. He saw food and suddenly he thought with his stomach. I didn't have a budgerigar; I had a food processing flying machine.

Hold on, how was this possible, how could he smell food from three rooms away? By now Peter had regained some sense of order and he got up and switched on the lounge room overhead light. That brought more pizza slices into the picture and Limpy instantly took flight and landed close to the pizza box. That was lucky because if he had landed on the pizza he could have burned his feet. Before he made another move Peter took the box away. "Thanks mate" I called out "that was quick thinking"

Limpy made it quite certain that he wasn't amused, screeching as he headed to his feed. If that bird talked he would have been swearing his head off. He hardly touched it but quite clearly was thirsty as he helped himself to a drink. He didn't want to know us as he flew onto the kitchen radio and stayed there.

When the beer, pizza and the TV programme had finished, Peter and I adjourned to the kitchen. Limpy hadn't moved off the radio. One look was enough to see that his head was lowered and he was struggling just to keep his eyes open. "Come on mate" I softly said as I brought my finger forward for him to step on, "time to go to bed". There was no argument from him. Limpy slowly stepped on my finger; I moved him close enough to step onto my shoulder and took him back to his sleeping quarters. I didn't even bother leaving the bedside light on. I'm sure that by the time I returned to the lounge room he was sound asleep.

One of my year's highlight occurred on the second weekend of February. On that weekend I headed north past Sydney and attended a function in the Chichester State Forest just past the town of Dungog. I have showed up without fail every year since 1978. This year was no exception. I gave my house keys to Marian my next door neighbour told Limpy to behave and departed on Friday morning.

As enjoyable as the road trip was, as enjoyable as it was to meet my mates from the previous year, as wonderful as it was to sit down around the camp fire and look up to a dazzlingly clear star studded sky I was actually counting the days to return back and make sure that Limpy was OK. I missed him; I actually had to admit to both myself and my mates that I was missing that flying mischief maker.

While I was enjoying a Chinese meal on Sunday evening I told my hosts that I had changed my mind and instead of staying the night would instead do a night run. Although they understood they made me promise that I would stop at the first sign of tiredness. I agreed.

Five hours later, lightning in the distance announced the coming storm. Hardly had I crossed back into my State when the heavens opened and the torrential downpour was the heaviest I had ever been in. Yawning and the idea of driving through the storm put an end to my plans. I pulled over and had a nap.

When I woke up I worked out my estimated time of arrival back home and was happy to know that I would arrive home before Limpy would wake up. "That's great," I spoke out loud "I'll surprise him". As I got back on the road I smiled as I realised that I would see my mate quite a few hours earlier than planned.

Noting the time when I drove up the driveway I didn't put the car in the garage, just gently opened the front door, tip-toed into the lounge room and settled down in my lounge chair. Glancing at the kitchen clock I was pleased that I had made it with some time to spare.

The first chirp signified waking up. From where I was positioned I was able to see Limpy fly out of the bathroom into the bedroom landing on the bed, and since I wasn't there, he flew off again into the bathroom. Time passed, I picked up a TV magazine and lazily turned over the pages. The sound of a pair of wings gave me just the split second time to lift my head up as Limpy came into view emerging from the bedroom. One short sharp whistle from me and instantly his direction changed as he unexpectedly spotted me sitting down. Let's face it when he left the bathroom for the first time in the morning he always saw me in bed and not in the lounge room. If an aeroplane pilot changed direction that quickly he would have piled up all the passengers into the tail section.

There was no doubt about it. He always placed a smile on my face - no wonder I loved him.

Limpy flew straight onto my shoulder. Immediately he started to fervently, loudly chirp and whistle in my ear. I loved it. Mind you for all I know he might have been telling me off for not being around, but to me that was music to my ear. He really was excited, unable to stand still, chirping even when he started grooming my ear.

Was I happy? His actions managed to moisten my eyes. It was an enjoyable, fun filled weekend but the return was a memorable one.

Well Limpy, your welcoming behaviour deserves a treat; you'll get a very light portion of vegemite at breakfast time.

I managed to spot my neighbour hanging out her washing so I waved to let her know that I had returned early.

A few minutes later I was enjoying a hot shower with Limpy standing on the shower screen frame intently looking down at me. "Don't worry mate, I'm not leaving" I chuckled.

As soon as I stepped out of the shower Limpy jumped on my head. Now I do not mind him on my bald head but I hate it when he uses his claws as a brake to slow him down. Shaving is a daily chore but quite unusual to see a bird moving about on my head as I moved it around. The next step after shaving was applying aftershave and this is where I started chuckling.

After I put on the aftershave Limpy started sneezing. There's a limit on how many times I say 'bless you'. This was the result of the alcoholic fumes from the aftershave. As it ascended he started breathing it and the end result is a bout of sneezing.

Limpy was one bird that didn't suffer from blocked nostrils.

Chuckling soon turned to uncontrollable laughing. Once I had finished I filled his drinking container. He soon flew down for a nice aerated drink. As he was still sneezing he lost his footing and fell head first in the drinking container. I had expected him to blow bubbles, he pulled his head up which was completely under water, shrieked an ear piercing scream and took off in a huff. Seeing Limpy on the bathroom radio with all his head feathers completely soaked, I did what every responsible owner does, broke into uncontrollable laughter. It looked like he was wearing a drooping moustache. He, on the other hand, was definitely not amused.

I walked into the bedroom and proceeded to dress. He definitely wanted to keep me in his sights. In the past he hung around me while I was dressing and this time was absolutely no exception. Sitting down on the bed was easy; putting on a pair of socks was an adventure in patience. He stayed on my foot and then dangled off the socks as I was putting them on. I told him "Mate, all I want to do is to just put these on". Imagine putting on a T shirt and feeling Limpy climbing across my back to my shoulder. There was no way I was going to escape.

As soon as I walked into the kitchen Limpy flew off me and 'reported' his early morning adventures to his mate in the mirror on top of the fridge. I carried out the normal morning inspection of his droppings plus changed the water and feed. Neil Mitchell talkback programme was on the radio, the kettle water boiling and all was well with the world. How was it possible that as soon as I retrieved the vegemite jar from the pantry Limpy stopped chatting to his mirrored mate? How could the sounds of vegemite being spread on sliced toasted bread causes him to run to the edge of the fridge? There was no need to call Limpy to the kitchen table, a simple wave of a sliced vegemite toast and he would rush over in the blink of an eye. If there was anyone in his way he would have bowled that person over.

Limpy should have been contracted out to do Vegemite TV commercials. You would think that he was glad to see me? Watch him behave standing a beak's distance away from his favourite food. I think 'behave' is the wrong word. He didn't nibble the vegemite; he devoured it as fast as possible.

At lunch time Marian popped over asking me how the trip went and also 'reporting' Limpy's behaviour while I was away. She said that like previous times Limpy got close to her when she dished out his food but as could be observed while I was present, she didn't count.

While I made us a cup of coffee Marian pointed out that the car was still in the driveway. I explained that when I arrived I didn't want to make any sound by opening the garage door and sneaked into the house to surprise Limpy. I said that I was aware of it and would shortly put it in the garage. She indicated that it would be better to put it away because in my haste to get out I had left the car keys in the ignition. "Oops," was my reply and hurriedly walked out to retrieve them. There was no way that Limpy was going to let me walk away; he came out of nowhere landing on my shoulder and firmly hung on. OK I'll pick them up later.

The afternoon was spent unpacking, laundry and doing a few chores, I might add with Limpy's constant supervision. I couldn't even go to the toilet without him being present. As expected, that night Limpy slept on my arm again.

Chapter 15

Limpy as usual woke me up. Looking out the window showed the promise of another beautiful day. This is the type of day that shouldn't be spent inside the house, the perfect day to go socialising.

Unfortunately the only person I was going to visit was my dentist and rest assured there wasn't going to be any socialising taking place there.

When Limpy wasn't looking, I sneaked out. I actually had to sneak out of my own house. As soon as I returned back home, I was rewarded by Limpy flying back onto my shoulder. He chirped out his usual greetings, however when I tried to whistle my numb lower lip failed me, no sound came out. Try as I might there was no way I could whistle. All I succeeded in doing was to make a half-hearted raspberry noise and dribble. Over the next hour or so Limpy would sit on my shoulder and chirp at me and expected a reply, no luck, it was a one way conversation. At times he flew away and returned a moment later, as if to try again, chirped expecting a reply, but there was no response. He definitely got frustrated because he let go a few high shrills guaranteed to blow my ear drum across the room. I did try, but nothing came out, my lips were out of action. I did laugh - he wasn't amused I'm sure.

When finally, I was able to feel my lips puckering, I did whistle. When that happened he turned, faced me and started to chirp and whistle again, thankfully at a far lower volume. I loved it, I just broke up laughing.

Regrettably summer, like all previous summers came to an end. Clouds once again appeared and the gloom and doom of winter would soon be upon us. That's how I saw it; Limpy didn't see it that way at all. He had discovered a new hobby. I learned what it was when I left an account on the kitchen counter instead of taking it to the study.

I tore open the envelope, shocked once again the see the rising cost of electricity and placed it on the kitchen counter, went into the study to retrieve the previous account for comparison. I was away less than a minute.

In that brief moment, Limpy flew over and proceeded to crinkle cut the edges. Showing up and calling out 'Oi' made no difference, he was busy leaving his mark. It didn't matter what type of account it was. He was exercising his artistic talent. Of course when I retrieved the account he wasn't happy and took off chirping out an ear piercing short sharp chirp back to the bathroom.

What I didn't know, what I could not have possibly foreseen was Limpy's new hobby, perhaps even a new love, the overwhelming joy of tearing paper. The roll of toilet paper never knew what had hit it. It was at his mercy.

Limpy had in the past used the toilet roll as a landing spot; it was easy to get too, soft on the legs and quite comfortable to crouch on. He had on a couple of occasions nibbled it leaving tell-tale signs of his presence, but all that was to change.

I had learned years ago that if Limpy wasn't flying around or arguing with his mirrored reflection or chirping/whistling than he was either having forty winks or up to something. That something is usually mischievous or possibly destructive.

A room to room search got underway. He must have sensed me coming because as soon as I walked into the bathroom he flew off the toilet roll landing on my shoulder and instantly started to groom my ear. It clearly was a case of g'day mate, nothing is going on here. I turned around and looked at his reflection in the bathroom mirror. If ever there was a look of guilt, it was now. Oh he was going hell for leather, he wasn't waiting around, he knew what he was doing and he wanted to get back in my good books.

I turned to look at him and instantly he started to groom the tip of my nose. This wasn't dedication; this was sucking up. A single step forward and I could see that Limpy had torn a deep hole in the toilet paper. Now this had happened once before but not to this destructive level.

Try and speak while a bird is grooming ones nose. "Well done mate," I said, "you have created a hole in the toilet paper. You know what that means don't you, I can't use it". I saw the roll slowly reduce in size as I continued unrolling ruined sheets.

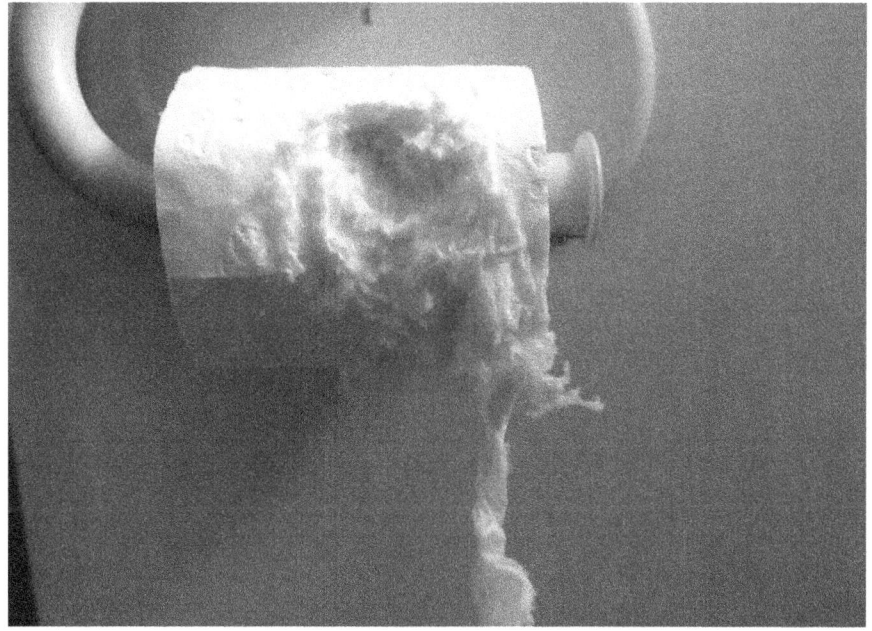

Limpy was here

Back in the kitchen I threw away the damaged sheets and returned to the study. Limpy didn't chirp or whistled once. As soon as I sat down he jumped onto the back of the chair and silently stayed there. At times I looked back, he didn't move a muscle.

It must have easily been twenty minutes before he let out a single chirp. A moment later he chirped again and shortly after finding no opposition he started chirping and whistling to his heart's content.

I had assumed that the incident was now closed, but boy oh boy, was I wrong. Limpy had discovered the joy of shredding toilet paper and there was nothing that was going to hold him back. Every time I realised that the house lacked noises then a certain flying misfit was busily converting toilet paper into an unrecognisable lump.

Still you have to hand it to him; as soon as I showed up he would instantly take off landing on my shoulder and trying his best to distract me from the sight of utter destruction.

He became more destructive, or should I say artistic when he tore a hole in the roll and then later actually turned the roll over and started creating another hole.

> When you have a bird flying around it is imperative that the toilet bowl lid is always placed in the closed position. The danger of a bird falling in can easily happen and once his feathers especially the flight feathers get wet he'll be unable to fly out and will drown within a few minutes.

As winter started to make itself felt, Limpy found new ways to destroy the humble toilet paper roll. No matter what I did if a toilet roll was visible to him then it died a horrible death.

There was a time where I was going to the visitor's toilet because I knew that the paper there was still usable. The on-suite bathroom roll once damaged was left as is and not replaced. When the roll was completely shredded to pieces and thrown away I left the holder empty. Another change of tactics, when required I left the roll on the cistern. It worked. Finally I didn't have to clean up the torn pieces off the floor and remove sheets until I come to the useable ones. Ah the joy of walking in the bathroom and not having to look and shake my head from side to side.

I said in Chapter 4 that my brother was obviously born in a tent because tents do not have doors and he never closed a door behind him. That hadn't changed; he left the visitor's toilet door open. So much for using that roll, only one flyby was required, Limpy spotted the unguarded roll and thoroughly, enthusiastically ripped it to shreds.

Accept the inevitable Frank, and just move on. That was the advice I was given so I bought a packet of the cheapest toilet paper and let him loose. I kept a roll aside on the window sill for my own use.

Life returned back to some sort of normality. After destroying and I do mean thoroughly dismembering three rolls in one day he was satisfied and started to ease off. I was glad because it started to become a rather costly issue. I was happier still when on one three day period no roll was touched.

That was the calm before the storm. That bird was lulling me in to a false sense of security.

Living with Limpy

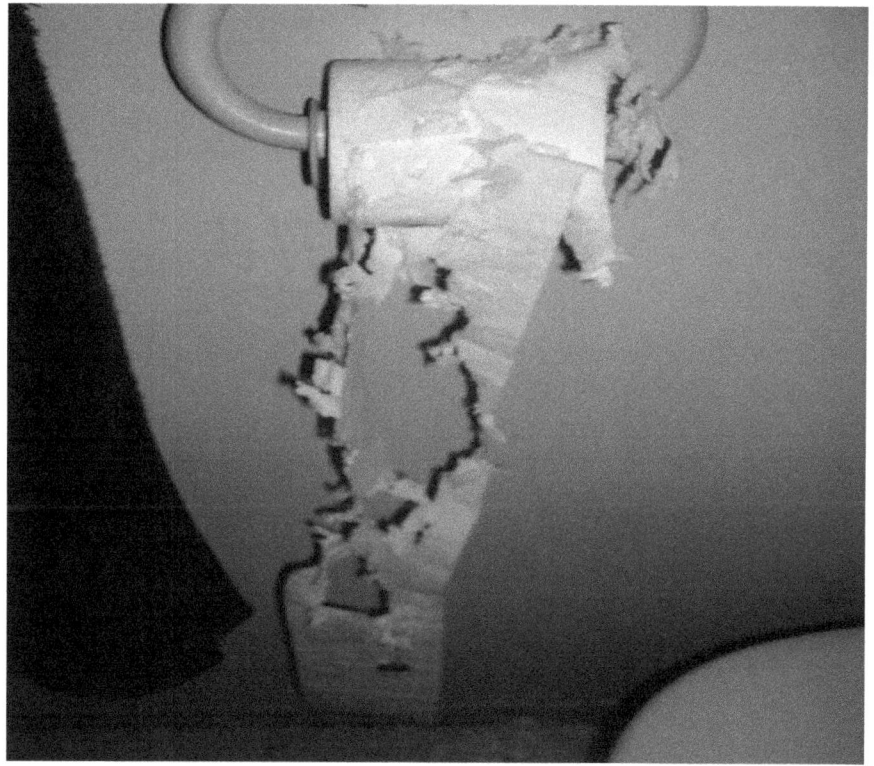

Limpy's artistic works

Every Monday morning Brenda, the carer came over to carry out certain chores. Over a cup of coffee pleasantries were exchanged before I retired to the study to let her do her assignments Shortly after I sat down at my desk Brenda came over and informed me not to go to the bathroom, pointing out that Limpy had "fallen of the wagon" He was back to his old tricks. He hadn't just holed the roll but literally unrolled it. "Unrolled it", I queried, "how does a bird unroll a roll of paper?' I cried out. "See for yourself" was the obvious reply. The bathroom floor was covered with the paper piled up on the tiles in picturesque disorder.

Limpy playing it safe flew onto the bathroom radio. Spinning round he looked down, enjoying his work. Turning to Brenda I asked her whether I should get a shot gun or a budgie whisperer. She just broke up laughing.

Later that night Limpy once again came out, briefly landed on my shoulder before helping himself to a late snack and a drink before returning back to me. He soon gave me the signal that he wanted to go back to the bathroom.

I made the mistake of switching off the bedroom light as soon as I left him. This resulted in him flying out, so once he settled down again, I left the light on and switched it off later.

So here I was approaching my 60th birthday and being dictated to by a budgie about when I should switch off a light - Aargh.

The End Result

The following morning one look at the bathroom was enough to just turn over and go back to sleep. Not happy that he had shredded the cheap roll of paper that I put out for him, he had also turned to 'my roll' of paper that I left on the window sill. He pushed it off the sill, let it roll out all the way till it stopped against the wall and started to shred it as well – Aargh, he's not a bird, he's a flying misfit.

Destroying paper became Limpy's number one passion but that didn't stop him from getting into anything and everything else.

It is always a joy to arrive home, whistle and have Limpy fly over to greet me. In this particular case that didn't happen. As soon as I walked into the kitchen I saw Limpy with his head inside an empty yogurt tub. Oh no, I had cleared the table, put everything on the kitchen sink to wash but somehow missed in throwing away the empty yogurt tub. No point in whistling at him, he was in heaven feasting. As I have already stated, I was positive that this bird lives to eat. When he finished he flew off onto the kitchen radio. While he was busy 'licking his lips' I was busy laughing as I looked closely at the tiny spots of strawberry yogurt all over his head, beak and neck. He's not able to clean the top of his head properly so when I finally cornered him I used a tissue to clean him up.

After I released him he ran up my arm, onto my shoulder and started to groom my ear. I didn't know whether he was getting back in the good books, or thanking me for cleaning him up.

I started to walk towards the bedroom so I could change. Usually Limpy would come along for the ride but there are also times when he flew off ahead. When he did that he flew onto the bedroom curtain rod, kept looking at my movements and as soon as I sat down on the bed he swoop down onto my shoulder. In this instance he flew off me and headed straight to the bedroom. On the spur of the moment, I decided to trick him.

Just before I left the dining room I doubled back and returned to the kitchen. I stood silently leaning against the kitchen counter looking towards the hallway. A few moments later I was practically doubled over with laughter. It couldn't have been done better if there was a script to follow. Limpy came over but instead of his usual high speed flight, he actually walked back. He was looking for me turning his head this way and that. Even though budgerigars show no facial expressions one could easily see him wondering "what happened?" This was funnier still because as soon as he spotted me he let out an enthusiastic single solitary chirp. How could one keep a straight face?

Keeping in mind that he was named due to his limp, he was unable to walk a straight line. Well he actually did but he had to change direction half way because wherever he aimed to be, his strong right leg caused him to always end up a few inches off course.

I had tears running down my face; I just had to sit down. When I got some strength back I walked over, bent down and while still laughing presented him with a finger to hop onto. He jumped on then flew to his favourite spot on the curtain rod and just stayed there looking at me. As for me, as I was changing my clothes, every time I laid eyes on him I broke up laughing again.

Back in the lounge room I settled down in front of the TV. Limpy briefly stayed on my shoulder before flying back to the bathroom. I knew the toilet paper roll was safe when I heard Limpy argue with his mirror mate.

A few commercials later Limpy flew back but this time he landed on the carpet, right in the middle of the lounge room. I didn't know whether to watch TV or Limpy walking about in his rather unique style. Eventually he walked over very close to my left foot and stopped. A few moments later he walked away and stopped directly in front of my right foot. Strange, what is he playing at? Next he moved away and jumped onto the left foot. A moment later he jumped off, walked and jumped onto the right foot. I just looked at him, what was he playing at? This rather strange behaviour was new. Next instant he let out a single, short, sharp and bloody loud shrill. I wondered, reached over and presented a finger saw him jump on. As I sat up he flew onto my chest and then walked up to the shoulder.

"You mean to tell me that you didn't feel like flying over, I had to pick you up? I don't believe this, is this getting back at me for tricking you?" I queried. Limpy looked at me, briefly groomed my ear and crouched down. A moment later he was asleep resting against my neck.

I think I had been outwitted by a budgie!

I returned to watching TV quite aware and enjoying his body warmth against my neck.

When Limpy woke up, he started to once again groom himself and stretch this way and that. It wasn't easy trying to watch TV with a wing feather in one's ear.

Once the grooming was over Limpy started to merrily chirp and whistle. He had the knack of making as much noise as possible just when the movie I was watching was getting quite interesting. So I increased the TV volume. The problem is that two can play at that game. Then just when the Chief Inspector was about to reveal who the murderer was, Limpy opened up his lungs. He had the capacity to be heard from across the road. Turning over and telling him to shut up didn't help. Yes he did briefly stop and look at me, but as soon as I turned my head away he started again. By this time the murderer had been revealed and I had missed out on who it was.

Aargh, he can be so infuriating. Clearly this is pay back for tricking him.

All was forgiven as a few days later his actions were side splittingly funny. At the height of winter I received a visitor, Darren who rode his motorcycle all the way from Sydney, approximately a thousand kilometres away. Keep in mind that Limpy had seen my family and friends who are mostly my own size, but Darren was the exception to the rule. This was the first time that Limpy had ever laid eyes on him. When he rolled up my in driveway, I went to greet him. When I walked back into the house Limpy did his typical loud chirping, high speed flight heading towards my shoulder. However as soon as my mate walked in behind me, Limpy executed the fastest U turn I have ever seen him do. Compared to my 5ft-5inches height, at 6ft-5inch and weighing just less than 300 kilograms, Darren is a giant of a man. He's a gentle giant, but to Limpy he positively towered over me.

Both he and I broke out laughing at Limpy's evasive action. As soon as we both sat down Limpy flew over and hid behind my neck. There was no way that Darren could hold a conversation without bursting out laughing. Every few minutes I could feel Limpy move to one side to see whether this man mountain was still there. Darren could see Limpy peeking out from behind my neck and then hide again, more laughter followed.

Limpy eventually accepted his presence however he simply refused to get off me, only doing so when Darren walked away and was out of sight. Limpy didn't have to hide for long as Darren was only passing through. Early the following morning after Darren waved goodbye, Limpy once again flew around the house without any walking mountains in the way.

Chapter 16

That blasted bird, oh, one of these days I'm going to tie his wings behind his back, blindfold him and offer him a last cigarette before marching him to the firing squad.

Years ago when my parents passed away I received their glass topped coffee table. I placed quite a number of photographs under the glass for any visitor's viewing.

Limpy, being Limpy did inspect it but hadn't bothered landing on it for quite a couple of years. Well to a degree it was directly below his flight path, there was no need to cut short his flight.

One morning as soon as I entered the house struggling with groceries, I did what I usually do, call out to him. No sound of flapping wings, no loud screeching, just silence. When that happened I knew he was up to something. By now I had learned of his selective deafness. As I walked into the lounge room I saw him walking around on the coffee table. That blasted bird wasn't looking at the photographs; his head was bopping up and down busily looking at his own reflection in the glass.

Off course he was playing it cool. And so he should, he had left quite a few droppings on the glass. I was not amused. He flew onto my shoulder and started chirping in my ear. He, most likely was telling me about his new mate.

I cleaned the surface with the same spray can agent as all the house mirrors. That same afternoon as I was sitting down in the lounge room Limpy once again came over and this time landed directly on the table. It was a perfect two point landing except the glass surface didn't offer any traction whatsoever and saw him skidding sideways without any control at all. Naturally at the end of the table he fell off the edge. Somehow more from good luck rather than good management he had enough height and with wings madly flapping managed to gain air speed and flew straight up to the curtain rod. It goes without saying that he loudly protested all the way. As for me, seeing his sideway antics was enough to go into fits of laughter.

From that moment on that surface was cleaned by simply using a wet sponge and some paper towel.

At the start of spring a number of celebrations took place. First it was the welcoming of the new season; soon the days not only got longer but more importantly warmer. To have a steel reinforced leg, this warmth is a blessing. But better yet I was able to walk using only one crutch. Suddenly I had a free hand; it was wonderful to be able to use it to grab items rather than just the crutch handle. I could see a marked improvement in my leg and strongly believed that by Christmas I should be able to walk either with a walking stick or unaided.

Spring also meant that Limpy turned five years of age. That didn't mean anything to him. He hadn't changed his outlook on life, human food was still number one priority, still waking me up and still having either chats or arguments with his mate in the various mirrors. He still annoyed the next door neighbour's cat. And when he had a free moment and I wasn't around, he still thoroughly enjoyed demolishing the toilet paper roll. I could have thrown a party with miniature streamers and party hats and a birthday cake but a birthday treat of toasted sliced bread with vegemite was all that he loved.

It's uncanny, there was Limpy sitting on the kitchen radio merrily chirping along with the music, but the sound of a toaster giving up its bread was enough for him to stop chirping, fly onto my shoulder and intently watch me spread some margarine on the bread. As soon as I opened the vegemite jar Limpy swooped down and was practically in the way of the knife. He emitted a shriek of protest as I took away the bread and placed it on a plate. As soon as I presented the plated toast watched him attack it.

Later in the morning I saw him eat some seeds and clearly noticed that he didn't devour them with the same enthusiasm as the vegemite. He certainly appreciated the vegemite treat. One thing that hadn't changed, when it came to eating was still as sloppy as ever.

Come lunchtime and I sat down in front of the TV with a coffee and a sandwich. Limpy having once again had a few seeds and a drink flew over and landed on my head. His landings would be more welcomed if he didn't use his talons as brakes on my bald head.

As soon as I got over the harsh landing I looked up and whistled. As soon as he replied I felt a sharp pain in my left eye. Immediately, I lowered my head causing Limpy to fly off as I placed my hand over the eye. No, it didn't help; it didn't take the burning pain away. Whatever I had, it was quite painful. With tears running down my cheek I went into the bathroom and tried to wash my eye. That and eye drops didn't help so I grabbed the car keys and drove straight to an optometrist.

After what seemed like hours but was only 10 minutes I sat down facing the optometrist in a small dark room. Tilting my head back he dropped a few drops of a yellow dye in my eye explaining that this would help spot the offending item. With the eyelid madly fluttering and my hands squeezing the armchair the offending item was spotted and removed with the help of cotton bud.

Inspecting what to me felt like a boulder, I was informed that all I had was a seed husk. "A seed husk?" I cried out, that blasted bird who never believed in cleaning up after had eaten has dropped a husk that was stuck near his beak, and this was the cause of all my pain. When asked how it came to be I explained to a very attentive optometrist what had taken place. He laughed before pointing out that this little adventure is going to cost me eighty eight dollars – aargh that blasted bird. I returned home, looking at everything with a yellowish tinge and a major dent in my wallet.

When I arrived back home, I could hear Limpy softly chirping and whistling in the bathroom. I should go and tell him off but what would be the point, all he would do was to fly over and start chirping in my ear.

Switching off the kitchen radio revealed my presence. A moment later I could hear Limpy's loud chirping followed by the beat of flapping wings. Next instant I saw him fly out from the bedroom speeding all the way towards me. He didn't land on me; he just used my body to bring him to a complete stop. He landed straight onto my chest and then climbed onto my shoulder. He was quite excited as he moved about on my right shoulder, chirping, whistling and grooming my earlobe. There was no point in my admonishing him; he was so vocal that the result was my ear drum starting to reverberate. In the bedroom he continued 'carrying on' as I changed my clothes. I knew that he was glad to see me but this was a more excitable welcome than previous ones. Did he know what had happened?

He took off flying back into the bathroom and I followed. Aargh - you don't want me to tell you what happened to the toilet paper do you?

For all I knew he was saying that he saved me from being attacked by the toilet paper.

That night for the first time in a long time I went out. So as not to disturb him I collected the right clothes and changed in the lounge room. When I returned back again so as not to disturb Limpy I undressed in the lounge room and using just the light from the mobile phone walked into the bedroom and slid into bed.

If I had walked and switched the lights on he would have woken up and most likely flown over. Then it would be a task getting him to turn in.

Limpy turned five. I reflected back on the day I brought him home. It just didn't feel like five years had passed. In that time I saw him grow into a rather unique character, show unexpected behaviour, and become a real mate to a lonely man who had spent empty days recuperating from two major accidents. There have been many incidents that I shall never forget, such as the first time I heard him replay my favourite whistle but the most outstanding, unforgettable moments were the times of greetings upon returning back home. A single whistle was all it took to hear loud chirping followed by the flapping wings as he flew halfway round the house and onto my shoulder.

At times he would fly towards me at speed and use my chest to stop his flight. He then would start climbing towards the shoulder to be followed by an ear grooming session.

Was it a birthday celebration or simply letting me fall into a false sense of security?

For about a ten day period Limpy had left the toilet rolls alone, then one sunny morning, as I yawned and stretched approaching the bathroom I saw him just finishing unrolling a complete roll of toilet paper onto the floor. There were no holes, no torn strips just unrolled. He didn't even seem flustered that I had caught him out. He just looked at the mess spread around the floor. Talking hadn't helped; placing the roll on the cistern hadn't helped either. What to do?

Maybe the time had come to take him to see a psychiatrist. Aargh blasted bird. Look at the mess.

This was again repeated the following morning. For some reason he decided that another unrolled toilet roll is a welcoming sight. There in living colour on the bathroom floor countless feet of toilet paper heaped up in picturesque disorder – aargh. Some people jump into the shower, others lather up for a shave, me, I sat down on the toilet bowl and started to roll up the paper into some sort of order – with a bird sitting on my shoulder supervising. An hour later I realised that I had forgotten to close the visitor's toilet door. You've got to be quick, but I wasn't. Limpy had left his mark. Another roll was unravelled.

Aha, I said I'll place a rubber band on the paper roll so that will prevent Limpy from unrolling it. He seemed to have a perverted pleasure to walk on the roll and watch it unroll.

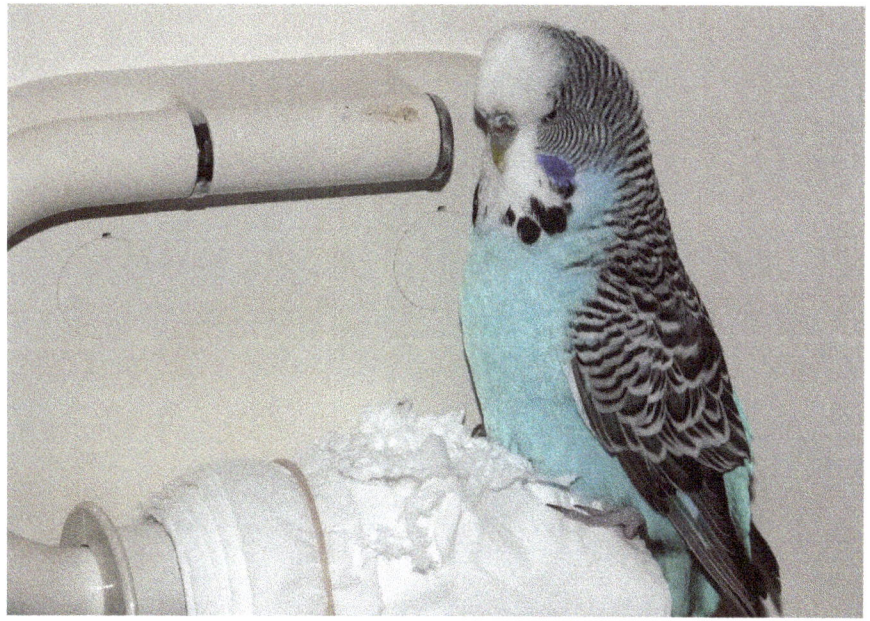

Don't look at me like that. The rubber band didn't help.

Should I accept the inevitable and just move on? I was yet to find out that worse was to follow.

In the past when I had walked into the bathroom and caught Limpy 'red-handed' tearing up the paper, he immediately flew over on to me and started to groom an ear. When a few days later it happened again, he instantly froze, still with the paper in his mouth. He looked at me wondering what was going to happen next. It was rather funny he didn't move a single muscle. A moment later he flew onto my shoulder and once again started his "G'day mate" routine.

Seeing that I took no action, the next few times I caught him out he literally ignored me and kept on tearing the paper. I didn't believe this, I actually approached him close enough to touch him and he still keep on shredding the roll. By the time he worked out that he could get away 'with murder' he started to tear up strips, take off with a strip in his beak and deposit them in the wash basin, on the bathroom radio, on the toilet seat, and even on the shower door frame. What is this, redecorating?

It goes without saying that Limpy's favourite pastime wasn't a pastime at all. It became an obsession. He was certainly attacking the paper with a vengeance.

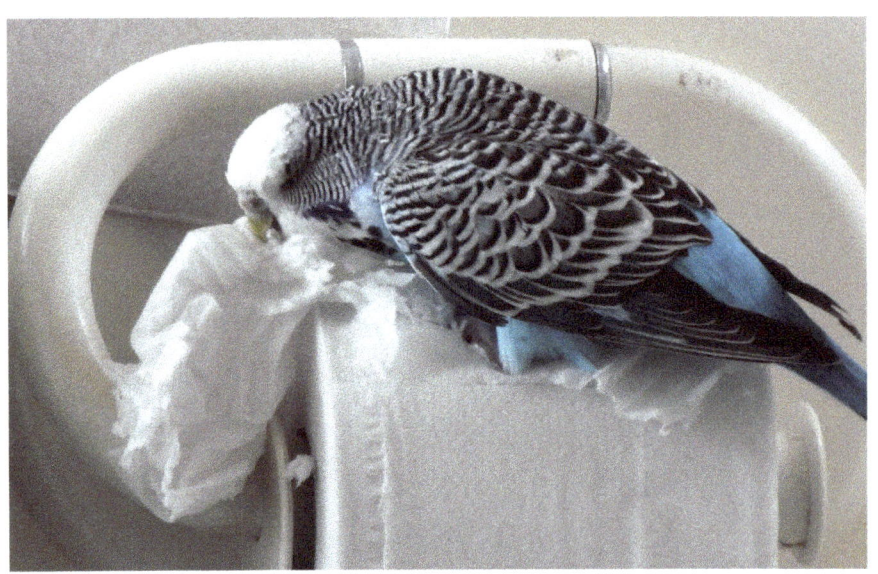

Don't mind me, mate!

I had tried to introduce toys for him to play with, to occupy his mind but it was a fruitless exercise. Toilet paper rolls were the go.

I believe that if a roll of paper was a living entity by the time Limpy had finished with it, it would have died. Perhaps an hour with a psychiatrist is a waste of time, I'm sure that time spent at a reform school would be better.

Living with Limpy

Meanwhile, time, physiotherapy and pain medication were the three ingredients that helped see me overcome my injury.

By the end of spring I had convinced myself that by Christmas I would be able to walk without a walking stick. To say I was happy would be an understatement. I started to venture out more often, the house no longer feeling like my prison.

With the visitor's toilet door closed and the bathroom toilet roll on the window sill, Limpy soon found other ways to amuse himself, arguing with his mate in the mirrors and annoying the cat were still on his 'to do' list. Mind you when I did forget to put away the rolls or when a visitor forgot to close the toilet door, Limpy saw the opportunity at hand. Upon my return one roll was disfigured and the opened visitor's toilet door meant that the other roll had died a horrible death.

I'm exhausted

At the start of summer I reflected back on how quickly time seemed to have passed. I told Limpy that October was the first anniversary of my road accident and on Cup Day in November was the second anniversary of when he tore his wing feathers. Now within the next few days I was very confident that I could take my first steps without the walking stick and in the last day of the year I would turn sixty years of age. There Limpy, you have just entered middle age

Living with Limpy

and I am about to enter retirement age. Looking at him for a response was disappointing; all I got was a tilt of his head to one side, and a silent look.

On Sunday the fourth day of December I nearly walked the length of the hallway unaided. You should have seen the look on my face. The last time I had walked unaided was in April 2007, fifty-six months ago.

Limpy was on the kitchen radio when I walked up to him, telling him what I had just achieved. "We should celebrate mate" I happily said out loud, "one ration of vegemite toast for breakfast tomorrow."

Budgies usually get millet as a special treat, Limpy had vegemite instead. No doubt about it, he was an Aussie all right.

Keeping through with my promise, on Monday morning we both sat down with a toast of vegemite sliced bread and I let him help himself – as if I could stop him. He dived straight into it, boots and all.

Later that day the house was quiet again. No, this time he wasn't attacking the toilet paper, he crouched down on the sofa, which was bathed in the afternoon sunlight and dozed off. I silently tip-toed away, returning back with the camera.

ZZZZZZZZZZZZZZZZZZZ

Chapter 17

The following Saturday with Christmas only two weeks away I woke up planning to go and do some Christmas shopping. Limpy didn't wake me up which was unusual and wasn't around whilst I shaved. Back in the bedroom while I was dressing I became aware that the house seemed unusually quiet. I hadn't heard Limpy usual chirping/whistling. I slowly stood up from the bed and still holding on to a sock, left to seek him out.

I looked for him everywhere getting quite concerned because I couldn't locate him. It was a relief to find him back in the bedroom sitting on some folded clothes placed on the chest of drawers. I briefly laughed relieved to see him, but suddenly concerned to see that he wasn't his normal standing tall. He was all fluffed up. I approached him, extended my finger and he stepped on. "What's wrong mate?" I softly said. I placed him on my shoulder and walked into the kitchen quickly replenishing his food dish. Shaking the container I spread the seeds evenly and put it back in its place. If the seeds weren't disturbed then that would tell me that wasn't eating.

I walked back into the bedroom and continued dressing. Limpy took priority so I decided that all planned activities/chores would be cancelled. After all I reasoned I still have plenty of time for Christmas shopping. I made up my mind that I would stay at home and keep an eye on him.

As the minutes passed by I could see that he wasn't his usual active self even when he walked around my neck from one shoulder to the other. I watched him like a hawk. He stayed on my shoulder and not once did he utter a single chirp. This was unsatisfactory, so I rang the vet and requested for Limpy to be urgently seen. I was glad to be told to pop over later that same morning. I sat down in the lounge room, aimlessly thumbing through a picture book just waiting for the right time to depart. I made myself a cup of coffee but hardly touched it. I offered him and he did accept a small drink, but no food at all.

Living with Limpy

Limpy didn't once chirp in the car. The trip to the vet seemed endless. In the waiting room he just stood still all hunched up. From past experience the only way to calm him down whilst in a cage was to let him sit on a finger. Not now, something was definitely wrong with him. I wondered what had happened. Thinking back to the day before, he had been his normal active self; he even succeeded in turning a perfectly good toilet roll into a misshaped useless lump of paper. Finally after what seemed like hours, we were called in and I anxiously handed the cage over to the vet.

Limpy was thoroughly physically examined including a micro examination of his droppings. She said that apart from being hunched up everything was fine however he might have a bacterial infection so for the next 5 days I was to administer some oral medication.

Although I was relieved to hear that all was well, his silence and hunched up position started to stress me. The slow moving Saturday morning traffic made me quite irritable. I hate to think how many times I sounded the car's horn as I gunned the engine hard, blindly overtaking traffic. It wouldn't have surprised me if I had attracted the police with my driving. I also wondered whether I had activated a speed camera.

Back in the kitchen I opened the cage door. Where in previous times Limpy would have shot out of the cage, this time he took his time and walked out onto my arm and made his way up to my shoulder. He stayed there until I opened the pantry door and brought out a loaf of bread. As soon as I placed it on the kitchen counter a single chirp was heard and a pair of flapping wings announced his presence.

Silly me; food was present. I laughed as once again I saw Limpy trying to work out how to get to the bread through the plastic wrapping.

Try making a sandwich with a budgerigar getting in the way. I could not move anything without him inspecting it. I reached over and presented him with his bowl of food. Limpy walked over, helped himself to a few seeds and returned back to my sandwich.

Just after finishing my lunch, Limpy flew to his bowl and helped himself to food and water. He was merrily chirping, he was back to normal. What happened this morning seemed so long ago? It was more like a nightmare as once again I enjoyed Limpy doing high speed fly-bys; spending time on my shoulder and visiting his mates in the mirror.

I sat in awe in the lounge room as Limpy flew quite low from the kitchen through the dining room and half way through the lounge room then he suddenly swooped up heading straight for and landing on the curtain rod. He has flown to the rod before but never from such a low position. I was impressed. He then surprised me by turning around and jumping off aiming straight towards me and in the last moment flapped his wings and settled down on my shoulder. I broke up laughing as he repeated his flight straight from my shoulder to the curtain rod, turned around and flew down back to my shoulder. What looked funny was his minute hesitation before he turned around on the rod. It looked like he landed asked "now what do I do" turned around and flew down. He looked like he was playing. I loved it.

I put my feet up, switched on the TV and relaxed by watching a movie, although that didn't stop me looking at him as he flew by.

Later in the afternoon while making myself a coffee I saw Limpy fly and land on the back of my lounge room chair and then fly and land on the coffee table. When I sat down with my coffee he flew over landing back on my shoulder. I whistled but he didn't reply. I suddenly realised that I hadn't heard him whistle or chirp for some time. I turned and looked at him just as he started to walk down my arm and jumped off landing next to my coffee cup. A moment later he settled down once again hunched up. "What's going on?" I spoke out loud. "Mate, please tell me that you're not sick again?" I started to worry as I reached over presenting my right index finger inviting him to climb on. Limpy looked down at the finger and with what looked like hesitation, slowly, very slowly stepped on. This took far longer, this isn't normal.

Alarm bells, loud alarm bells, started to ring.

I felt a cold sweat and momentarily held my breath. I didn't know what was happening. I re-positioned myself on the chair. Without knowing why, I felt a sickening feeling. I found myself lowering my voice when I asked him what's wrong. Opening my left hand I brought Limpy across and he slowly stepped over and crouched in the palm of my hand.

I felt a lump in my throat and had trouble speaking. "Oh God, mate, what's happening to you, is this it?" I whispered, "Is it time to say goodbye?" Limpy lifted his head and looked directly into my eye. He had in the past made numerous eye to eye contacts but this was different, he never broke eye contact. I slowly, very slowly started to caress him moving my index finger along the outside of the wing. This went on for some time. I hit the mute button on the TV plunging the room into complete silence; the only sound was my whispering, thanking him for his friendship, his companionship, his teachings and his antics that had had me in stitches.

He suddenly moved up my hand then tilted his head, lowered it, resting against my thumb. There was no eye blinking, he once again looked directly at me, took one more long last look; then slowly his eyes closed, forever. His head then marginally dropped.

Limpy had silently passed away.

The silence in the room was deafening. Stunned, I just looked at the still body, having trouble comprehending what had just taken place.

I slowly caressed him one last time, gently running my finger along his back all the way to the end of the tail. His legs were neatly tucked in, the left one which gave him his name, still as deformed as ever.

"So long, mate", I croaked "you can now rest in peace. Have a safe journey and look out for me at the Rainbow Bridge" I murmured. I gently put him down, walked into the bedroom and closed the door behind me.

As the sun set I aimlessly walked about, the TV still in silent mode. I switched on the computer informing my family and the internet Budgie Group what had taken place. I lost my appetite and ended spending the evening alternating between staring at the TV and the computer monitor.

I shed a tear for my mate. It was so sudden, so unexpected. At 3.57pm he stepped on my finger and passed away at 4.07pm a mere ten minutes later.

He was just under 5 ½ years old. He was middle aged.

For the first time in a very long time I switched on the main light when I entered the bedroom. I switched on the bedside radio just to make a sound. Limpy was gone, there was no one to disturb or wakeup.

It was a long lonely disturbing sleep, I kept waking up.

The following day, no one woke me up and when I did the house sounded so empty, so quiet, and so desolate. It was the passing of something. Something had changed and will never be the same again.

As I lay in bed I once again could hear the kitchen clock slowly ticking. I hadn't heard that for years. It was eerie entering the bathroom; there was no one to greet me. Limpy's chirp accompanying my electric razor and his daily bout of sneezing following the application of aftershave were missing. When I finished from the bathroom I switched off the radio. The house was still.

I emptied and put away the feed and water containers plus the portable mirrors. I originally didn't want to but as the morning progressed I ended ringing the vet regarding having an autopsy carried out. The vet was so surprised with the news and agreed to me bringing him over as soon as possible. She too wanted to know what had happened. Without realizing it I checked to make sure the house was safe before I drove over.

On the way to the vet I saw three lorikeets fly overhead. As beautiful as they are, the last thing I wanted to look at was birds.

As soon as I arrived at the vet, the receptionist came over and wanted to know what had happened. She started stressing out as I told her. An elderly woman in the waiting room put down her magazine and came over asking questions. As soon as the vet came out, without uttering a word she just held and hugged me. She said that she knew the strong bond we had and had spoken about it on quite a number of occasions with other bird lovers. She said that the couple with the most vocal budgie on her patients list wanted to meet Limpy. She than asked me to describe what had happened. The autopsy would be carried out as soon as the office closed down for the day. She said that from what I had described she might have an idea. I queried if Limpy had a heart attack and she said no that would be the least problem because she had felt his muscles, heard his heart, he was in excellent condition.

On the way back home I saw another three beautiful lorikeets passing overhead. I mindlessly wondered whether they were the same three I saw before.

Just after lunch the vet rang me and told me what had taken place.

Limpy had passed away due to an abdominal tumour. Upon examination it was found the abdomen was full of blood. She said that the good news was that he was never in any pain. Once it ruptured there would have been a massive loss of blood and he would have briefly slipped into unconsciousness before death.

She said Limpy knew that something was wrong; he had just enough time to say his goodbye. Because of the strong bond between us the sudden down turn also meant that I knew something was very wrong and likewise had just enough time to say goodbye, before the end.

At dusk I switched on the computer plus the study and kitchen radios, increasing the volume rather high as if to drown out the eerie silence.

Emails of condolences and phone calls came thick and fast from Australia, America, Canada and Britain. So many emails, some so beautifully written, it overwhelmed me and once again found myself shedding a tear.

Sleep, once again, didn't come easy.

Monday morning dawned bright and sunny; I opened the bedroom curtains and looked out the window, it showed the promise of a beautiful day. It was another new day, another new week and shortly, another New Year. Time was moving on. I turned around looking directly into the bathroom at the now empty towel rack, Limpy's favourite sleeping spot.

I felt sadness, emptiness that I had felt a few times in my life. And yet, at that same moment I also started to reflect on the 5 ½ years of laughter I spent with a budgie named Limpy, for now he had moved to live in my memory.

For here had been a budgerigar whose love, loyalty and friendship went above and beyond the call of duty.

The End

Living with Limpy

September 2006 – December 2011.

Rest in Peace mate

Postscript

From that fateful day onwards I never saw Dobbie the Siamese cat on the kitchen windowsill.

A week after Limpy passed away I received a condolence message which certainly gave me food for thought – "Limpy entered your life shortly before your accident that crippled you; before you couldn't walk and left just after you were able to. Was Limpy a guardian angel looking over you while you were in a dire strait?"

As a memorial I bought five plants, one for each year Limpy was with me and planted them in the back yard. Each plant is an Australian shrub that attracts wild birds.

www.ingramcontent.com/pod-product-compliance
Lightning Source LLC
Chambersburg PA
CBHW050832010526
44110CB00054BA/2652